CLASSIC BRITISH MOTORCYCLES
OF OVER 500 cc

CLASSIC BRITISH MOTORCYCLES
OF OVER 500 cc
From The National Motorcycle Museum

Bob Currie

Patrick Stephens

First published in 1988

British Library Cataloguing in Publication Data

Currie, Bob, *1918-*
    Classic British motorcycles of over 500cc
    from the National Motorcycle Museum.
    1.   British motorcycles, to 1984
    I.   Title
    629.2'275'0941

ISBN 1-85260-083-7

Patrick Stephens Limited is part of the Thorsons Publishing Group, Wellingborough, Northamptonshire, NN8 2RQ, England.

Printed in Great Britain by
Butler & Tanner Ltd, Frome and London

10   9   8   7   6   5   4   3   2   1

Contents

Introduction — The Big Stuff   7
1925 799 cc AJS Model E1   10
1960 646 cc AJS Model 31   12
1927 996 cc AJW Summit   14
1936 597 cc Ariel Square Four   16
1962 696 cc Ariel Straight Four (Prototype)   18
1913 770 cc Bat No 2 Light Roadster   20
1923 598 cc Beardmore Precision   22
1930 998 cc Brough-Superior SS100 Alpine Grand Sports   24
1932 797 cc Brough-Superior Austin Four   26
1938 996 cc Brough-Superior Dream   28
1954 646 cc BSA A10 Golden Flash   30
1963 646 cc BSA Rocket Gold Star   32
1971 654 cc BSA A65FS Firebird Scrambler   34
1914 744 cc Clyno 5–6 hp   36
1928 998 cc Coventry-Eagle Flying Eight   38
1981 992 cc Hesketh V1000   40
1939 592 cc Levis 600   42
1923 678 cc Martinsyde Six   44
1933 592 cc Matchless Model B Silver Hawk   46
1936 990 cc Matchless Model X   48
1930 680 cc Montgomery Greyhound   50
1964 646 cc Norton Dominator 650SS   52
1965 800 cc Norton P10 (Prototype)   54
1975 850 cc Norton Commando Interstate Mk III   56
1984 588 cc Norton Wankel Interpol Mk II   58
1954 598 cc Panther Model 100   60
1983 850 cc Quasar Four   62
1921 699 cc Raleigh Model No 9   64
1939 1,140 cc Royal Enfield Model K   66
1961 692 cc Royal Enfield Constellation   68
1917 976 cc Royal Ruby 'Russian'   70
1913 750 cc Rudge Multi   72
1938 986 cc Scott Model 3S   74
1935 649 cc Triumph Model 6/1 Twin   76

1950 649 cc Triumph 6T Thunderbird   78
1960 649 cc Triumph T120 Bonneville   80
1975 744 cc Triumph T160 Trident   82
1937 998 cc Vincent-HRD Series A Rapide   84
1955 998 cc Vincent Series D Black Shadow   86
1950 998 cc Watsonian-JAP (Prototype)   88
1912 848 cc Wilkinson-TMC   90
1913 964 cc Williamson Flat Twin   92
1928 680 cc Zenith 'Six-Eighty'   94

Introduction ... The Big Stuff

Tell a present-day youngster that Royal Enfield used to build a vast 1,140 cc vee-twin (as they did indeed, in the period just before the Second World War) and his likely reaction will be. 'Did they have Superbikes then?' But wait a minute! Whatever the situation today, in bygone times a big engine did not necessarily imply a scintillating performance. After all, an ox is one of the most powerful animals on earth, but I would not give much for its chances if entered for the Epsom Derby! Likewise, that big vee-twin Enfield mentioned a moment ago was more likely to be seen on weekdays hauling ladders and builders' merchandise around — or on a Sunday at the seaside, hitched to an ornately-painted ice cream float.

It was not so much what big bikes did, as the way they did it. On sheer speed, a lumbering side-valve twin could probably be beaten hands down by a fussy overhead-valve single of less than half its capacity. But the thing was that the internals of the smaller model were being stressed to the limit to produce the performance. On the other hand, the bigger engine would be turning over at a very low rate, its internals so lightly loaded that it was likely to last forever.

Naturally, they were not all like that, and yes, certainly there were glamour machines around. Switch on a mental image of a Brough SS100 (Lawrence of Arabia owned a string of them over the years, should you care to add mystique to glamour); and what comes to mind is a wind-up gramophone playing a record of *Valencia*, plus-fours and silken cravats, and a summer's day picnic beside the lazy waters of the Cam or Isis. And did anyone ever see a Coventry-Eagle Flying Eight at any time when it *wasn't* haring off at great speed bound for the Brooklands paddock?

But generally it was the fate of the over-500 cc motorcycle to spend its life as a sidecar haulier. Very few families could aspire to a Morris Cowley, and so something big but sedate, attached to a big, open sidecar with a luggage rack at the back, was the norm, at least until 1923 anyway, when the little Austin Seven began to increase in numbers. This car did to some extent woo paterfamilias away from three wheels, but not as extensively as might have been imagined, and it was not until the early 'fifties and the advent of Alec Issigonis's minor miracle car, the Mini, that the sidecar-makers really began to feel threatened.

The motorcycle, you see, had quite a lot in its favour. Buying a car was an all-at-once experience, but gravitating from a solo to a sidecar outfit was a gradual thing. In his courting days, let's say, Pa already owned a bike, and to transport his intended around on days out, all that was needed was a cushion to strap to the rear carrier (though later legislation would insist on provision of 'a proper pillion seat securely attached to the machine'). With marriage in the eventual wind, the ceremony would be both human and mechanical, for in addition to Pa, the bike itself would be joined in matrimony — probably to a sporty single-seater open sidecar. That was not too much of a strain on the financial resources; the bike was there already, and all Pa had to buy was the sidecar and chassis.

Later, as his business prospered, he could well decide to go upmarket, to a more powerful machine and a more luxurious sidecar (though, like Nora Batty of *Last of the Summer Wine*, there were many housewives condemned to trundle around at 20 mph in a battered chair hauled by a decrepit BSA). When children arrived, the single-seater body would be exchanged for a child-adult to fit the same chassis; in time, maybe, there would be an enormous saloon Busmar.

In the 1920s especially, should Pa happen to have been a small trader, there were further advantages to the sidecar outfit, since the commerical use of the combination was widespread. Telephone linesmen used them, while Shell had a fleet of outfits for their petrol-pump service engineers. Sidecar bodymakers were happy to produce special advertising outfits, so you found box bodies shaped like a crusty tin loaf; The Lodge plug company had a machine the body of which was in the form of a sparking plug; A Bromsgrove shoe shop delivered their customers' purchases with the aid of a sidecar beautifully crafted in aluminium into the shape of a boot — laces, eyelets, and all.

Now this was fine for weekday work, but what about weekend leisure? Well, the beauty of a sidecar was that detachment from the chassis meant just undoing perhaps four bolts, so it was a relatively quick job to take off the commercial body, and drop a passenger body into place (there were some sidecar makers, such as Dorway, who actually advertised a swap-body system).

But don't run away with the idea that all motorcycles over 500 cc were intended to lug sidecars around, because there have always been enthusiasts who wanted to answer the call of the open road, with as much power as possible at their command. Matchless knew that well enough, and they expressly advertised their 990 cc Model X vee-twin of the late 'thirties for long-distance solo work, as having the short wheelbase and handling qualities of a single.

Sadly, it never went into production (Hitler had a lot to answer for), but at whom was the four-cylinder, shaft-drive Brough Superior Golden Dream aimed? Not at the family sidecar man, that's for sure. No, there were status-symbol seekers about, even then, and had the Golden Dream been introduced as intended, you would probably have seen examples parked outside golf clubhouses up and down the country each Sunday morning.

In post-war times the British motorcycle industry was very much under the influence of Triumph who, late in 1937, had launched Edward Turner's masterpiece of a vertical twin, the 5T Speed Twin (followed a year later by the Tiger 100 sportster from the same stable). So when the factories started production again after the wartime traumas, everybody wanted to add a vertical twin to their ranges; so we had Ariel, BSA, AJS, Matchless and Norton all trying to dip their bread into the gravy.

Funnily enough, all these newcomers were 500 cc, like the original Triumph, because to the conservative-minded British motorcyclist of the time, that offered power enough and to spare. But the immediate post-war years had also brought a tremendous export drive, especially to America, where characteristically, everything had to be king-size, and so they demanded and kept on demanding power and still more power. Now, there was a very good reason for limiting the vertical twin to 500 cc, for the design has an inherent end-to-end

crankshaft couple, and if you go over 500 cc, vibration becomes noticeable. Still, if the Americans wanted bigger engines, bigger engines they had to have. So the British twins grew to 600 cc, 650 cc, and even 750 cc in response.

A rather better solution was the in-line three as represented by the BSA Rocket Three and its cousin, the Triumph Trident. Be it said here and now that these were very good motorcycles indeed, but they happened along just a mite too late. Aided by wins in the prestigious Daytona races, the BSA-Triumph Threes achieved a spectacular reception on the American market and for a while they sold very well, but they had too short a time space in which to make their mark, because the Japanese had been working on four-cylinder models and these now took over.

By the 1970s the British motorcycle industry had all but collapsed, and many a brave name had gone to the wall. But all was not quite lost. From the wreckage Norton was salvaged, to produce the Commando twin, with an engine-mounting system which was claimed to absorb the vibration of an 850 cc vertical-twin (well, forwardly-inclined-twin) engine. Norton are still with us today, producing in small quantities the Norton Interpol Mk II police model with its twin rotary-piston Wankel engine.

There was even a late arrival on the motorcycle scene, when the Hesketh was launched with a fanfare of trumpets. This was a completely new overhead-camshaft vee-twin thousand, to have been built in Daventry. But it seemed the fanfare was a bit premature, for gearbox faults showed up immediately, and the machine was taken off the market until the bugs had been shaken out. The wait was too much for the strained finances of the company, and Hesketh crashed almost as flamboyantly as it had arrived. The factory auction was not the absolute end of the Hesketh, and the machine struggled back into penny numbers production (though maybe 'penny' numbers is quite the wrong description, for a machine as fabulously expensive as this one) in the stable block of Lord Hesketh's country mansion bordering Towcester racecourse. Nominally, anyway, it is still available today.

No, I haven't forgotten the vee-twin Vincent-HRD (which, towards the end, dropped the HRD suffix because the Americans thought it was some sort of a Harley-

Davidson; they were actually the initials of Howard R. Davies, who had founded the original marque!). This was a bike devised and manufactured by enthusiasts for enthusiasts and, in the immediate post-war days, was advertised as 'The World's Fastest Standard Motor Cycle (this is a fact, not a slogan)'. If not truly a Superbike in its present-day meaning, it was indeed a super bike which had a following of its own and sold quite well. It was, however, hampered by being built during the period when motorcycles were still considered second-class transport, and a maker dare not put a price label on a machine which reflected its true worth and gave promise of a fair return of profit.

The age when bank managers and middle-aged company executives would be seeking to regain something of their lost youth, by purchasing something elite for occasional recreational rides, was still some way off. If only Vincents could have hung on for a few more years — or better still, if only somebody could have acquired the manufacturing rights and reproduced the range a few years later — we might still have had Vincents parked on the forecourts of country mansions, instead, of BMWs.

In the book which follows, you will find details of 43 highly-assorted motorcycles, every one of which can be inspected at the National Motorcycle Museum at Bickenhill, near Birmingham. Even at that, it is but a taster of the many hundreds of bikes on display, but at least it offers a broad picture of the over 500 cc world. There are twins both vee and vertical, three-cylinders, and fours from very different periods of time. Nor have we forgotten the traditional big single, for no survey of big British bikes could possibly overlook that highly individualistic Yorkshire tyke, the Panther.

Many of the pre-war and just a few of the post-war models are vee-twins, perhaps the most handsome arrangement of cylinders ever dreamed up; and practical with it. 'Mankind,' averred George Brough, and he should have known if anyone did, 'has a natural partnership with the vee-twin. Its slightly offbeat exhaust note awakes folk memories, for it is akin to the hoofbeats of a galloping horse, and man and horse have been partners since the dawn of time.'

Each machine is beautifully portrayed in colour through the lens of Jim Davies. Study the pictures, absorb the wide variety of specifications, and marvel that just one comparatively small section of industry (and for all their international reputation, the British motorcycle manufacturers were never really massive employers of labour) could have produced such an imaginative array of ideas.

Bob Currie, Birmingham

1925 799 cc AJS Model E1

There always had been a vee-twin engine in the AJS range — even before there were such things as AJS motorcycles! In the early 1900s the Stevens Motor Manufacturing Company had been established to manufacture proprietary engines for the infant motorcycle industry, and the Stevens range included a hefty vee-twin which was supplied to Clyno (a make we will meet a little later in this book).

But the four Stevens brothers — Harry, George, Jack and Joe — soon felt the urge to go into motorcycle making on their own account, and by 1911 the new firm of A.J. Stevens had been established abandoning the old Stevens name and, instead, using the new AJS trade mark. Legend has it that only Jack (actual name, Albert John Stevens) had three initials in his name, and the four brothers felt that a three-initial monogram looked better on a tank than just two initials.

The manufacturing rights of the earlier vee-twin engine were sold off to Clyno, along with the former Stevens factory at Pelham Street, Wolverhampton, and the new enterprise began in works at Retreat Street. For the first year, AJS concentrated on a single-cylinder side valve, but at the 1912 London Show the first AJS vee-twin appeared. This was the 698 cc Model D side valve, with the cylinders arranged at 50°.

From the start, chain drive was specified, and although the front wheel initially had a cycle-type stirrup brake, a drum rear brake was fitted. From 1915, interchangeable wheels were fitted, and by this time the company had moved to bigger premises at Graiseley Hill, Wolverhampton.

Post-war, the Model D returned, now fitted with a somewhat angular saddle tank and with engine capacity increased to 748 cc. One-piece cylinder heads and barrels also been replaced by detachable cylinder heads retained in place by a cross-strap and tie-bolts.

However, the AJS big twin did not reach its full flowering until 1925. It had now become the Model E, and engine size had gone up again, this time to 799 cc. For the 1925 season a completely new frame had been designed, with a dropped top tube to permit a low seating height, and a hefty forged-steel gearbox mounting bracket.

Internally, the engine now featured the latest type of roller big end bearings while, for 1925, light-alloy pistons were quite a novelty; each piston carried three narrow top rings, plus a scraper ring at the base of the skirt. The Model E came in standard and de luxe versions, the latter embodying totally-enclosed chains and a Lucas Magdyno electric lighting set, whereas the standard version made do with chain guards and no lights.

The twin was designed expressly for sidecar use and was in fact catalogued as a complete outfit with an extremely roomy single-seat touring sidecar of the maker's own construction. However, it was used also for commercial work. In the years ahead, the AJS twin would grow still more, eventually to 990 cc, production coming to an end on the outbreak of the Second World War. Well-loved, the machine possessed outstanding hard-wearing qualities, was particularly flexible in operation, and was regarded as one of the sweetest-running and quietest models on the market.

Specification

Make AJS. **Model** Model E1. **Engine** 799 cc (74 × 93 mm bore and stroke) 50° side-valve vee-twin. **Tyres** 700 × 800 mm beaded-edge, front and rear. **Frame** Brazed-lug tubular construction, unsprung at rear. **Front forks** Brampton Biflex, with vertical and fore-and-aft movement. **Brakes** 6 in diameter drums, front and rear. **Weight** (solo) 326 lb. **Wheelbase** 55 in. **Manufacturer** A.J. Stevens (1914) Ltd, Graiseley Hill, Wolverhampton.

Above Total enclosure of the primary and final-drive chains was a worthwhile luxury feature. Note the early Lucas Magdyno electrics.
Right Cast aluminium footboards and swept-back handlebars gave the rider a majestically relaxed riding position. The speedometer is driven from a pinion on the front hub.
Far right The method of holding down the cylinders, by a strap over the head and tie-bolts, was AJS practice right through the '20s.
Below There was an air of supreme elegance about the big AJS range leader, a favourite with family sidecar enthusiasts. Note the imposing Tan-Sad pillion seat.

1960 646 cc AJS Model 31

One-make loyalties die hard! The trade-mark and manufacturing rights of AJS had been acquired from the defunct A.J. Stevens company as long ago as 1932, and in post-Second World War years Associated Motor Cycles, who now made both AJS and Matchless in their Plumstead factory were indulging in 'badge engineering' to such an extent that (apart from differences in finish) AJS and Matchless were nearly identical. Nonetheless, there were still many enthusiasts who would buy and cherish something with an AJS name on the tank, while sneering at the equivalent Matchless, and vice versa, of course.

But be that as it may, Plumstead had joined the swing to vertical twins as soon as was practical after the return of peace, with a 500 cc design from the drawing board of Phil Walker. Unlike every other British twin, this one used the old Silver Hawk idea of incorporating a centre main bearing in an attempt to rid the design of inherent vibration by making the crankshaft stiff. It was never wholly successful.

As time went by and AJS and Matchless machines hit the USA, so there came the inevitable cry for more power, which meant a bigger engine. So AMC obliged by boring the cylinders out to 592 cc. They could not go any bigger, because they were limited by the distances between the centre lines of the cylinders. Yet the Americans still weren't satisfied; they demanded even bigger twins.

There was only one remaining path to be taken. Since the bores could not be enlarged, extra capacity had to be gained by lengthening the stroke, making it 79.3 mm, instead of the 72.8 mm of the original 498 and 592 cc twins.

That in turn meant having to make a new crankshaft, and so the opportunity was taken of extending the drive side of the shaft so that it would accommodate a Lucas alternator (and that meant a new and very sturdy cast-light-alloy primary chaincase). The general dimensions of the crankcase were altered only slightly, and a distributor was fitted behind the cylinder block, in the position previously occupied by the magneto.

At first, the new 646 cc twins (Matchless G12, or AJS Model 31) were reserved for export only, production beginning in September 1958 for the 1959 season. This was but an interim measure, and for 1960 — and it is an example from this production year that we see here — there was a considerable amount of redesign, the major feature of which was an entirely new full-cradle duplex tubular frame. For the engine there was a new cylinder head which afforded the same compression ratios as before, with reduced valve angles. To assist the flow of cooling air across the head, an additional horizontal fin incorporated three small diagonal fins on its underside. Two-rate valve springs were specified.

As has been mentioned, AMC's famous centre main bearing never did succeed in taming engine vibration, so a different approach to the problem was made, by making the crankshafts from a higher grade of nodular iron. However, the Plumstead factory was running into difficulties, and by the end of 1961 the range of models was being slashed, the remaining mounts being 'jazzed up' by replacing the small and distinctive little tank badges by huge chromium-plated die-castings that would have been more at home on café juke-boxes. As the 'sixties ran on, so Plumstead production disintegrated into a pick-and-mix of Norton and AMC frames and engines until the end came in 1969. But by then the AJS Model 31 had long disappeared.

Specification

Make AJS. **Model** Model 31. **Engine** 646 cc (73 × 89 mm bore and stroke) overhead-valve vertical twin. **Tyres** 3.25 × 19 in front, 3.50 × 19 in rear, wired-on. **Frame** Brazed-lug duplex tubular cradle incorporating swinging-arm rear springing with hydraulic damper units. **Front forks** AMC hydraulically-damped telescopic. **Brakes** 7 in diameter front and rear. **Weight** 396 lb. **Wheelbase** 55¼ in. **Manufacturer** Associated Motor Cycles Ltd, 44/45 Plumstead Road, Plumstead, London SE 18.

Above Phil Walker was the man responsible for the discreetly attractive AJS vertical twin. It departed from normal practice in having a three-bearing crankshaft assembly.

Right Redesign to incorporate a crankshaft-mounted alternator brought the benefit of a sturdy cast-alloy primary case.

Far right Two bulges, covering the camshaft ends, distinguish the AJS timing chest. Inside the cover, however, the timing gear was identical to that of the Matchless G12.

Below 1960 marked the end of AJS's conservative look.

1927 996 cc AJW Summit

Believe it or believe it not, but the AJW motorcycle venture was something of a sideline to the still-flourishing Exeter business known as the Wheaton Printing Company. The AJW initials stood for Arthur John Wheaton (better known as Jack Wheaton), and the first few prototypes were assembled in the maintenance workshop at the printing works.

Motorcycling was Jack Wheaton's hobby, and the first two AJWs, built in the summer of 1926, comprised a 496 cc single powered by a Swiss-made MAG engine, and a powerful-looking 996 cc vee-twin using a British Vulpine power unit. In fact British Vulpine, and Summit, were alternative names for the big British Anzani engine, and when AJW production did begin the 1927 season it was with a modest range of vee-twin models, using the 996 cc overhead-valve Summit, and side-valve and overhead-valve JAP.

The AJW was certainly a very racy-looking machine, with its bulbous torpedo-shaped fuel tank raked back, and employing a full duplex tubular loop frame with the top members running in a straight line from steering head to rear wheel spindle. The machine seen here was the standard sportster, employing single-port cylinder heads, but there was also an even more imposing device, with twin-port heads and two exhaust pipes along each side of the bike. Its top speed was claimed to be around 100 mph, which could well have been true. The AJW not only looked expensive, but *was* expensive, with the top-of-the-range version costing an awe-inspiring £145. Even the standard model, as pictured, was priced at £115.

Naturally, the make attracted an elite clientele (among them Brooklands racers such as Claude Temple and Joe Wright) and production ran at a low level — which, as a hobby project, suited Jack Wheaton admirably. But even hobbies have to earn their crust, and as Britain ran into the depression years of the 'thirties, so the character of AJW changed. The last big British Anzani vee-twin (by this time available in racing specification only) dropped out of the range in 1931, and only a 680 cc vee-twin JAP represented the breed for 1932.

Nevertheless the make carried on right through the 1930s, by this time using single-cylinder overhead-valve JAP and Rudge engines (one model, the 1933 AJW Flying Fox, employed a Rudge Ulster unit in super-sports trim), supplemented by utility models powered by Villiers two-strokes. But Jack Wheaton was losing interest, and by 1937 the make had passed to other hands.

The final pre-war range announced for 1940 comprised a 500 cc JAP, and two versions of a 250 cc Villiers. But AJW was not finished, and in post Second World War years the make returned, with small-scale production of a vertical-twin side-valve JAP, supplemented by speedway and grass-track models. The failure of JAP to produce proprietary engines suitable for motorcycle use hampered AJW, as indeed it did Cotton and several more of the smaller British manufacturers, and in the 1950s and 1960s the make drifted into marketing 50 cc and 125 cc Italian-made ultra-lightweights carrying 'AJW' tank badges. It was, you might say, quite a comedown after such exotic beginnings! But at least the company lasted until 1981, outliving many bigger rivals.

Specification

Make AJW. **Model** Standard twin.
Engine 996 cc (78 × 104 mm bore and stroke) overhead-valve vee-twin Summit (British Anzani). **Tyres** 3.50 × 19 in wired-on. **Frame** Brazed-lug duplex tubular cradle, unsprung at rear. **Front forks** Druid side-spring girders. **Brakes** 8 in diameter at front and rear. **Weight** 320 lb. **Wheelbase** 56 in.
Manufacturer AJW Motor Company, Friernhay Street, Exeter.

Above Exeter was the unlikely home of the sporting AJW big twin, the initials standing for Arthur John Wheaton, member of a famous printing family.

Right The bulbous torpedo tank slopes down to give a fashionably low riding position. Front forks are side-spring Druids.

Far Right A 996 cc overhead-valve engine by Summit, of Willesden, London, gave the AJW a very lively performance. The magneto is driven by bevel gears.

Below The AJW make was surprisingly long-lived, fading out in the early 1980s with small Italian-powered sportsters.

1936 597 cc Ariel Square Four

Modern technology has long since found the solution, of course, but in the years leading up to the Second World War housing a four-cylinder engine in a motorcycle frame was quite a problem. Mount it lengthwise, and the machine's wheelbase was almost unmanageably long (for example, look at the Wilkinson, later in this book). Mount it crosswise, and the bike was unacceptably wide.

Matchless found one answer by evolving the narrow angle vee-four Silver Hawk, then a London dealer–designer–rider named Edward Turner thought up another; why not arrange the cylinders two by two — a sort of pair of vertical twins, one behind the other? The story goes that he scribbled the bare bones of the idea on the back of a cigarette packet, took the train to Birmingham, and tried to arouse interest in one factory after another.

BSA were nearly tempted, then got cold feet. In the end it was Jack Sangster, boss of the Ariel works, who decided to give the scheme a go. He found Edward Turner an office, gave him a junior draughtsman as an assistant (none other than Bert Hopwood, in later years to become a top designer in his own right), and told him to go ahead.

The result was the 500 cc Ariel Square Four which, by a coincidence, made its public debut at the very same Olympia Motor Cycle Show of 1930 as did its arch-rival, the vee-four Matchless. For convenience, the Ariel company mounted the new engine in the same duplex-down-tube frame already in production for their 500 cc sloper single, and a pleasant little job it was, too. But riders (especially sidecar men) felt that something a bit bigger than 500 cc was needed so, obligingly, the makers upped the capacity to 600 cc while retaining the original layout of two crankshafts geared together in the middle, with the rear crankshaft extended outwards on the left-hand side to carry the primary drive. Drive to the overhead-camshaft mechanism was, as before, by a chain on the right.

Shown here is the National Museum's 1933 model, and for that year a fair bit of redesigning had been undertaken. Instead of a separate oil tank, there was now a new crankcase assembly incorporating an oil compartment. A single-plunger oil pump driven by an eccentric delivered lubricant to the geared crankshafts, while surplus oil overflowed into troughs into which the big ends dipped.

Also new for 1933 was a single-down-tube frame with a duplex engine cradle and (at extra cost) a new four-speed Burman gearbox with positive-stop foot change. The combined effect of the redesign work was said to have cut the weight by a hefty 25 lb and the wheelbase by $1\frac{1}{2}$ in, resulting in a marked improvement in steering and road-holding.

Nevertheless, the overhead-camshaft Square Four was not the out-and-out success that the company claimed, the main snag being insufficient air space between the cylinder head and the underside of the cambox assembly. As those who tried to hot-up an Ariel for speed attempts (such as Ben Bickell did at Brooklands) soon found, the cylinder head tended to overheat and warp, and in consequence the engine developed an insatiable appetite for cylinder-head gaskets. They got over that eventually — by redesigning again, this time as a pushrod-ohv engine; but that was later.

Specification

Make Ariel. **Model** 4F Square Four. **Engine** 597 cc (56 × 61 mm bore and stroke) overhead-camshaft double vertical twin. **Tyres** 3.25 × 19 in wired-on, front and rear. **Frame** Brazed-lug tubular semi-cradle construction, unsprung at rear. **Front forks** Ariel centre-spring girders. **Brakes** 7 in diameter drums front and rear. **Weight** 370 lb. **Wheelbase** $54\frac{1}{2}$ in. **Manufacturer** Ariel Works (JS) Ltd, Grange Road, Selly Oak, Birmingham 29.

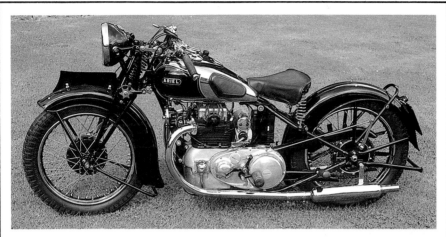

Above Primary drive is taken from the end of the rearmost crankshaft, the two shafts being geared together centrally in this design.
Right Black-and-chrome finish was an alternative to the more familiar Post Office red, and lent a special elegance to the model.
Far right Chain drive to the overhead camshaft is housed in the vertical casing. Carburettor on this model is front-mounted.
Below Early-type Ariel Square Fours employed a neat overhead-camshaft engine, originally of 500 cc but later of 600 cc. Flared and valanced front mudguard was continued into the 1950s.

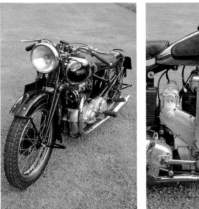

1962 696 cc Ariel Straight Four (Prototype)

Take an in-line four-cylinder ohv engine, and lie it on its side so that the cylinders point towards the left-hand side. Now, add a shaft final drive to the rear wheel, and you arrive at .... a BMW. But would it surprise you to learn that Ariel had been working on just such a layout a decade before BMW tumbled to the idea? In fact, the 696 cc was the very last project to come from the drawing-board of veteran designer Val Page, who had stayed at work well past retirement age to see it through.

There is a lot to be said for a laid-down straight four. For a start, it results in a low centre of gravity, with a consequent dramatic improvement in the handling. Valve gear is readily accessible from the left, and a detachable cover plate allows equally ready access to the big end and main bearings from the right. If the engine is set squarely in the frame, then the crankshaft is automatically offset from the longitudinal centre-line, meaning that there is a straight-line drive to the rear wheel bevel gears.

But *why* a straight-four? Well, the Ariel factory at Selly Oak had long been famous for the Square Four, and since that had now gone out of production a more modern four seemed a natural successor. It was not by any means easy because the Ariel works were members of the BSA group, and although they displayed a certain degree of sturdy independence, general manager Ken Whistance had to fight the parent company every step of the way.

BSA thought the straight four would be too costly to develop and put into production in the current economic climate of 1959; but crafty Ken Whistance had something up his sleeve. A straight-four engine of this size would be useful in the military field for powering a portable generating set, so if only he could negotiate an Army contract for Ariel, then he could charge the development costs to the military, leaving the factory with a nice little motorcycle engine at a bargain price.

The plot nearly worked, too; the British Army did show interest until the government of the time made a hefty cut in the military estimates. Later on, the Greek Army nearly bought the idea, but it was not to be, and in fact only one prototype engine was ever built — the one now exhibited at the National Motorcycle Museum in what looks for all the world like an Ariel Leader frame.

But look again; at the twin headlamp assembly on the front of the fairing; at the odd raised tailpipe of the left-hand exhaust system; at the longer-than-standard pressed-steel pannier boxes at each side of the machine. The styling is certainly based on that of the 249 cc twin-two-stroke Ariel Leader, but the sheet metal of the box-beam frame and trailing-link front forks is much more substantial in view of the extra power that the four was expected to push out. Fork stanchions are actually 16 gauge steel and their suitability for the purpose was tested by fitting them to a 1,000 cc Square Four.

On the test bed, in undeveloped form, the 696 cc four produced an encouraging 24 bhp, while on the road it was taken up to 80 mph with more to come. Alas, after about 400 road-test miles the one-off crankshaft distorted and wrecked the main bearings. By then, anyway, it was clear that the machine would never reach production. The BSA group decreed that Ariel was uneconomic and would have to close, and the four was put into cold storage.

Specification

Make Ariel. **Model** Prototype. **Engine** 696 cc horizontal in-line ohv four, with integral synchromesh gearbox and shaft final drive. **Tyres** 3.25 × 17 in front, 4.00 × 16 in rear. **Frame** Welded steel pressings, with swinging-arm rear suspension. **Front forks** Trailing link, in pressed-steel stanchions, with hydraulic damping. **Brakes** 6 in diameter drums, front and rear. **Weight** Not known. **Wheelbase** 57 in. **Manufacturer** Ariel Motors Ltd, Grange Road, Selly Oak, Birmingham 29.

Above The raised exhaust tailpipe hints that the bike is not what it appears!

Right The twin headlamp assembly is a distinguishing feature. Steel body and fork is Leader-style, but of heavier gauge material.

Far Right Power unit is a 600 cc straight four on its side, with the valve gear on the left.

Below A nicely-restored Ariel Leader two-stroke? Far from it, for in this case looks are deceptive.

1913 770 cc Bat No 2 Light Roadster

There are those who will argue until they are blue in the face that the BAT initials result from the manufacturer's famous sales slogan, 'Best After Tests'. In fact, it is the other way about. The Bat was the creation of Mr S.R. Batson and took *its* name from *his* name. That was in 1902, and in the next two years Mr Batson claimed to offer the first machine to the public without auxiliary pedalling gear, the first British bike to have a vertically-mounted engine within its frame, and the first successful spring frame.

It was not strictly a spring frame as we know it today, though it did afford the pioneer rider some insulation from road shocks. In fact the saddle and the footboards were coupled in such a way that they moved in unison, and were sprung from the main frame diamond. From the start Bats plunged into the competition world, and their initial successes were achieved with high-mounted, short-wheelbase models operating on cycle racing board tracks, such as Crystal Palace and Herne Hill. Engines used were imported De Dion singles, and the successful riders included the Chase brothers and T.H. Tessier.

However, after a couple of years Mr Batson decided to move into another line of business (office equipment, actually), selling out the motorcycle side to T.H. Tessier in 1904. By this time, S.T. Tessier (son of T.H.) was also riding Bats in competition, and it was from this that the 'Best After Tests' slogan was concocted. Unlike his father, S.T. Tessier was principally a sidecar driver, using a very special Bat at Brooklands with a water-cooled single-cylinder ohv JAP engine. But he was no slouch as a soloist, either, as he proved by finishing eleventh in the 1913 Senior TT at 43.83 mph, on a Bat equipped with both internal-expanding and external-contracting brakes operating on the rear wheel. Countershaft gearboxes were already becoming relatively common by 1913. Even Bat themselves offered one on their No 3 heavy twin, advertised rather oddly as the 'Pullman Car of Motor Cycles', but Tessier's Isle of Man racer, in the interests of lightness, made do with an Armstrong three-speed rear hub.

Indeed, the same arrangement of direct belt drive to an Armstrong three-speed rear hub can be seen on the No 2 Light Roadster which forms part of the National Motorcycle Museum collection. It has to be said, however, that Bat design was beginning to look distinctly old-fashioned in the final years before the First World War. Motorcycle production halted in wartime, with the works at Penge, Surrey switching over to making munitions. With the return of peace Bat failed to make much of an impression on the new motorcyclists and indeed, it was not until 1919 that the first post-war Bats were on offer, and opportunities had been missed.

But other firms were also in trouble, and Bat's takeover of the struggling Martinsyde company was hardly the best move they could have made. A result of the merger was the Bat-Martinsyde of 1924, featuring a Martinsyde vee-twin engine in a Bat spring frame. The public were not impressed, and after a few more desultory years the factory shut down its production line in 1927.

That was not quite the end of Bat, and for several more years, right into the early 'thirties, the works at Penge continued to offer spares and service facilities for owners of Bats and Martinsydes. Then that, too, petered out.

Specification

Make Bat. **Model** No 2 Light Roadster. **Engine** 770 cc (76 × 85 mm bore and stroke) 50° vee-twin JAP. **Tyres** 2½ × 26 in beaded-edge, front and rear. **Frame** Brazed-lug tubular diamond, unsprung at rear. **Front forks** Bat pivoted-loop. **Brakes** None at front, rear contracting band. **Weight** 220 lb. **Wheelbase** 54 in. **Manufacturer** Bat Motor Manufacturing Co. Ltd, 2 Kingswood Road, Penge, Surrey.

Above 'Best After Tests' was the sales slogan, but the Bat name was actually derived from that of the company's founder, S.R. Batson. The factory was at Penge, near Croydon, but production never recovered from the First World War.

Right Front suspension was Bat's own, and featured a pivoted loop.

Far right JAP engines were employed almost exclusively, except in the post-War Martinsyde merger.

Below Even for 1913, use of an Armstrong three-speed rear hub and direct belt drive gave a rather out-dated appearance to a model with a racing ancestry.

1923 598 cc Beardmore Precision

From a start in 1910, F. E. Baker Ltd rapidly gained a reputation for the excellence of the proprietary engines which they sold, under the Precision trade mark, to the motorcycle and cyclecar industries. Indeed, they were so successful that they became a very serious rival to the JAP concern. Moreover, orders came flooding in to such an extent that the original factory in Newtown, Birmingham, became much too small, and a new works was erected adjacent to the railway at King's Norton. That factory still stands, but the owners today are the world-famous Triplex Safety Glass Company.

During the First World War Frank Baker's concern was heavily involved in the production of munitions, but in odd moments some thought was put into what the Precision works would build when peace returned. Initial indications were that they would be back in the proprietary engine field, and in January 1919 details were revealed of the first post-war Precision engine, an all-new 350 cc two-stroke with automatic lubrication and the oil supply carried in the sump.

Behind the scenes, however, Frank Baker had been working on a complete motorcycle to be sold under the Precision name, a machine which broke away from tradition in a number of ways. One such change was the use of the petrol tank as part of the frame structure, while other features were leaf springing at front and rear, and externally contracting band brakes on both wheels. The machine was revealed in the motorcycle press of the day in October 1919, but when the doors of the first post-war Olympia Show were opened just a month later, it was seen that the name on the tank of the new bike was not Precision, but Beardmore Precision.

The explanation was that Glasgow ship-builders, railway engine and aero engine makers, William Beardmore & Co Ltd had taken a large financial share of F.E. Baker Ltd. Frank Baker continued on the board as managing director, but the chairman was Sir William Beardmore in person, and Beardmore's also had two more directors taking a hand in things.

The 350 cc two-stroke was the first machine to carry the Beardmore Precision label, but the range was soon expanded to include four-strokes from 250 to 600 cc. There was even a 349 cc with a sleeve-valve Barr & Stroud engine, built by the Glaswegian firm which had supplied gunlaying equipment for Beardmore-built warships.

However, the machine seen here is the 598 cc side-valve single, listed as the Model C. Nominally it was a $4\frac{1}{4}$ hp model, and the sales brochure remarked that 'By fitting a $4\frac{1}{4}$ four-cycle engine of 600 cc capacity to the all-steel spring frame Beardmore Precision, the machine has moved into the front rank of motorcycles for heavy-duty touring purposes, whether solo or fitted with sidecar'.

Designed by T.J. Biggs, the engine was really a revamp of the pre-First World War 598 cc Precision unit, but given unit construction by incorporating a Sturmey-Archer three-speed gear cluster within the main castings. Oil was carried in a compartment of the timing chest, and was circulated by means of a rotary sliding-vane-type oil pump.

The post-war 598 cc, claimed Precision, was 25 to 30 per cent more efficient than the pre-war version, and it was more silent, and more sturdily constructed. It may well have been, for it was to remain in the catalogue right to the end of Beardmore Precision in 1925, the final models being updated by the use of Webb girder forks.

Specification

Make Beardmore Precision. **Model** Model C. **Engine** 598 cc (89 × 96 mm bore and stroke) side-valve single in unit with three-speed gearbox. **Frame** Composite pressed-steel and brazed-lug tubular, embodying laminated leaf springing at front and rear. **Front forks** Pivoted at fork crown. **Tyres** 26 × $2\frac{1}{2}$ × $2\frac{1}{4}$ in beaded edge. **Brakes** 8 in diameter external-contracting, front and rear. **Weight** 285 lb. **Wheelbase** $54\frac{1}{2}$ in. **Manufacturer** F.E. Baker Ltd, Precision Works, King's Norton, Birmingham.

Above Not the prettiest
machine of its time, perhaps,
but one of the most
comfortable.
Right Front springing is unusual
and involves an L-shape leaf-
spring assembly. Handlebar
controls are roller-lever, not
cable.
Far Right The side-valve engine is
built in unit with a three-speed
Sturmey-Archer gear assembly.
Oil is carried in the sump.
Below Birmingham built, but
financed by a Glasgow
shipbuilding firm, the Beardmore
Precision broke new ground in
many ways. The tank is integral
with the frame.

1930 998 cc Brough-Superior SS100 Alpine Grand Sports

Top model in the Brough-Superior 1930 catalogue, the SS100 Alpine Grand Sports was billed as 'The Machine for Express Speeds with Armchair Comfort' — the 'Armchair Comfort' bit presumably referring to the cantilever rear springing system in which the whole of the rear subframe was pivoted (as it was also in the Vincent, Matchless Silver Hawk, and New Imperial, to name but three) under the control of friction-damped springs below the saddle.

To continue quoting from the catalogue ... 'Its ability to tick over in top gear at 10 miles per hour with scarcely a sound, its flashing acceleration and its effortless surging power output at all speeds, must be experienced to be properly appreciated. It is an 8/50 hp job having roller bearings throughout ...' and so on, and so forth. The words were almost certainly those of master showman George Brough himself, but perhaps the '8/50 hp job' will need a spot of explanation in these modern times. In fact, in early days there was a 'nominal horse power' method of classifying engines, whereby 2¾ hp was roughly 350 cc, 3½ hp was 500 cc. By this scheme, 8 hp equalled 1,000 cc, but 50 hp was the actual bhp output of the engine. So, 8/50 was a nominal 8 hp producing an actual 50 bhp.

The Alpine Grand Sports originated in 1925, when it was decided to produce a sort of super-SS100, the JAP factory having gone into production with a sports engine based on feed-back from Bert Le Vack's race successes. The new JAP was of 985 cc with triple valve springs and had roller bearings throughout. To complement the power unit, Brough's devised a new lighter and shorter frame, with Bentley & Draper rear springing, Castle leading-link front forks, and wheels (mounted on knock-out spindles) running on ball journal bearings. The fuel tank, in this early version, was nickel-plated.

Thus far the new model did not have a catalogue name, but George Brough entered the machine for the Alpine Trial, in which he not only made fastest time of day in the Katzburg Hillclimb, but put up the best performance in the whole trial. So Alpine Grand Sports! What else, indeed?

As the years passed, there were improvements in both the engine and in the Alpine GS as a whole. By 1930, when our example was built, the pushrods were enclosed in tubes, and there were covers over the rocker gear (though the valves still operated in the open air) and the valve mechanism was automatically lubricated. The machine specification embraced a stainless-steel fuel tank holding four gallons, and a special Sturmey-Archer gearbox with chrome-vanadium shafts and pinions. The box was a three-speed close ratio design, offering 3.5, 5.2 and 8.2 to 1 overall.

The Alpine Grand Sports was to remain in the Brough range until 1935 and in its later form it had acquired a foot-change gearbox, and a 998 cc engine delivering a hefty 74 bhp. This was the 'two of everything' engine, with two magnetos, two carburettors, full dry-sump lubrication, and mammoth bearing surfaces everywhere, and George Brough added a personal note in the catalogue, declaring 'I consider the new SS100 is the most thrilling batting iron I have ever ridden.' But then, he would say that, wouldn't he?

'Have you ever seen such a handsome bike,' asked George, writing about the 1934 Alpine Grand Sports 'so massive, so powerful, yet so small and compact? Its luxurious, effortless, road-gobbling qualities are almost beyond belief...' He would say that, too!

Specification

Make Brough-Superior. **Model** SS100 Alpine Grand Sports. **Engine** JAP 998 cc (80 × 99 mm bore and stroke) 50° overhead-valve vee-twin. **Tyres** 3.50 × 21 in front and rear. **Frame** Brazed-lug tubular cradle, with cantilever rear springing. **Front forks** Castle (Brough) leading link. **Brakes** Drums, 6 in diameter front, 8 in diameter rear. **Weight** 400 lb. **Wheelbase** 58 in. **Manufacturer** George Brough, Haydn Road, Nottingham.

Above 'Have you ever seen such a handsome bike?' asked the manufacturer, writing of the Alpine Grand Sports. He certainly had a point!
Right Based on a Harley-Davidson design, the leading-link front forks are of George Brough's Castle make.
Far right A handsome polished shield covers the bevel-gear-driven Lucas Magdyno. External oil pump is a Pilgrim.
Below Taking its name from a success gained by George Brough in person in the international Alpine Trial, the SS100 Alpine Grand Sports was the flagship of the range in the early 1930s.

1932 797 cc Brough-Superior Austin Four

In the days when second-hand Austin Seven engines could be bought from scrapyards at about £1 apiece, it used to be quite a widespread hobby to build a water-cooled four-in-line special; the OEC factory would even build you an Austin-powered four (but then they would build *anything*) to order. But only one British factory ever achieved what passed for series production of such a model and that was Brough-Superior. Mind you, a total production of just ten machines was not exactly up to present-day standards!

Announced in 1931 and catalogued for 1932 only, the Brough Four did not use the standard Austin engine. According to George Brough, it used a 797 cc unit, built exclusively for him by special arrangement with Sir Herbert Austin. Well, perhaps; but it seemed to be just the standard 747 cc Austin Seven, bored out by 1.9 mm per cylinder, and topped with a light-alloy cylinder head. The increase in capacity was supposed to boost the power output — but, said *The Motor Cycle* at the time of its introduction, it should be emphasized that the machine to which it is fitted is not designed purely as a speed mount, but as a luxurious passenger outfit, which will attain a speed of something better than a mile a minute and maintain almost that speed for as long as road conditions permit'.

The engine was not the only novelty. There was also an Austin gearbox, with shaft final drive to a bevel box with a wheel each side of it. Twin rear wheels would certainly have made the machine hard to handle in solo form, but Hubert Chantrey proved that it could indeed be ridden solo by taking a machine through the Land's End Trial. Use of the Austin box meant that it also had a reverse gear, something with which playful Brough Four sidecar riders were wont to alarm those not in the know.

The example shown in the National Motorcycle Museum's collection is *not* one of George Brough's original ten, but is a clever representation by Albert Wallis of one of the series known to have been cut up in an Anglesey scrapyard, the starting point being a spare rear bevel-box casting which still existed at the Brough works. Albert already owned a Four himself, together with a number of parts including a pair of radiators, and a standard Austin Seven engine and gearbox, and so with a great deal of hard work and ingenuity he was able to construct the museum's machine as a replica of his own model.

According to Hubert Chantrey, building the prototype model had cost George Brough £1,000 in 1931 — in present-day values, something in the region of £50,000. Catalogue price of the production version, complete with a launch sidecar of Brough's own design and make, was £188, which was actually cheaper than a rigid-frame SS100 vee-twin equipped with the same sidecar with a catalogue price of £200.

The factory's record cards exist in the hands of the Brough Club, and strenuous efforts have been made to chart the history of the ten models known to have been made, but two have never been traced. There are two survivors in the USA, another in New Zealand, four are still in Britain, and — counting the one scrapped in Anglesey — that was the lot.

A fulfilment of George Brough's dream it may have been, but 1932 was one of the deepest of the Great Depression years and there just wasn't the money about, particularly when you could buy an authentic Austin Seven car for £70 less than an Austin-powered Brough outfit. It just didn't make economic sense.

Specification

Make Brough-Superior. **Model** Straight Four. **Engine** 797 cc (57.9 × 76 mm bore and stroke) water-cooled, in-line four-cylinder side-valve Austin. **Tyres** 3.50 × 19 in front, twin 3.00 × 19 in rear, wired-on. **Frame** Brazed lug tubular cradle, unsprung at rear. **Front forks** Castle leading-link. **Brakes** 8 in diameter drums, front and rear. **Weight** (solo) 510 lb. **Wheelbase** 59½ in. **Manufacturer** George Brough, Haydn Road, Nottingham.

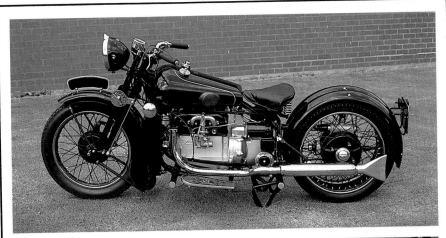

Above Only ten Brough-Austin Fours were made, and the history of most is known.
Right Twin radiators are well separated, so that they project into the air flow.
Far right The Austin engine, claimed George Brough, was specially bored out by 50 cc. Normally, it would have had a cast-light-alloy cylinder head.
Below Not only the engine, but also the gearbox is of Austin Seven origin. Crown wheel and pinion assembly at rear necessitates twin rear wheels.

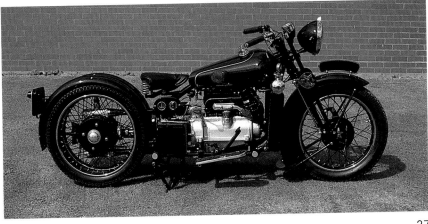

1938 996 cc Brough-Superior Dream

In his time, George Brough produced a whole series of show-stoppers, but the one which created the biggest sensation of them all was the transverse flat-four, shaft-drive Dream (or as some called it, from its metallic gold finish, Golden Dream), which was first exhibited at the Earls Court Show of 1938.

In essence, the design was a team effort involving George Brough himself, the flamboyant Freddie Dixon, and Ike Hatch of the Blackburne company (who had also been responsible, in part, for the Excelsior Manxman and, later, the AJS 7R racer). As first conceived, the engine was a pair of flat-twins, one above the other and with the crankshafts geared together. The camshafts, too, were gear-driven and in its initial form the cylinders had square dimensions of 68 × 68 mm bore and stroke.

However, in the course of development work, a redesign was decided upon, and a completely new version of the four emerged. Now the bore and stroke dimensions were 71 × 63 mm; and while the crankshafts were still geared together, the camshafts were chain-driven. A gearbox was bolted to the rear of the engine unit, with the drive being taken from the lower crankshaft. Final drive was by shaft to a wormwheel and underslung worm at the rear axle.

The frame was a wide-splayed tubular cradle, with plunger-type rear springing, while front suspension was looked after by the usual George Brough Castle leading-link forks, derived from a Harley-Davidson design. The fuel tank was massive, holding 4½ gallons of petrol, but in addition a door in the lower side of the tank revealed a tool-carrying cavity.

Mounted on a platform above the gearbox and driven from the rear end of the upper crankshaft was a special Lucas magdyno, with a distributor built into its forward end. Gearbox design was not really finalized, for George had both three-speed and four-speed boxes manufactured to his own design by David Brown's of Huddersfield. Four or five prototype Dreams were built, no two being exactly alike; some had a conventional kick-starter, but others featured a hand-starting

lever, and it is this last design which can be seen on the Museum's exhibit.

With appetites whetted by the 1938 Earls Court Show presentation, would-be customers waited — and waited — but there was no sign of a production Dream, though George Brough made encouraging noises in the press from time to time. Indeed, a pre-production model with a four-speed instead of three-speed gearbox was put in hand, to be ready for the 1939 Earl's Court Show; but that was the show which never took place, war having been declared in the September. The Brough-Superior works where the 'Rolls-Royce of Motor Cycles' had been produced was switched to the making of components — ironically, for Rolls–Royce themselves — for the wartime aeronautical expansion, and they were destined never to return to motorcycle production.

What happened to the other prototypes is not known, but just two Dreams are known to have survived — a black one, in the hands of a prominent Brough Club member, and the one shown here, the gold-finished model which was the actual 1938 Earl's Court Show exhibit. The selling price was to have been £189, astronomic by 1939 standards, so goodness only knows at what a post-war Dream would have been priced!

Specification

Make Brough-Superior. **Model** Dream. **Engine** 996 cc (71 × 63 mm bore and stroke) transverse flat-four overhead-valve with geared crankshafts, shaft final drive. **Tyres** 3.50 × 19 in front, 4.00 × 19 in rear. **Frame** All-welded tubular cradle, with plunger rear springing. **Front forks** Castle (Brough) leading-link type. **Brakes** Drums, 8 in diameter front, 9 in diameter rear. **Weight** Not known. **Wheelbase** 58 in. **Manufacturer** George Brough, Haydn Road, Nottingham.

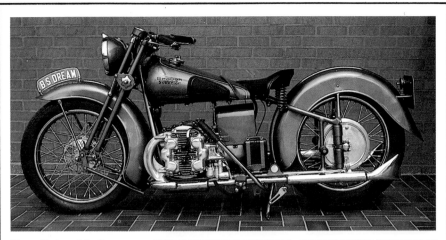

Above Design of the Dream was never finalized, and several variants were tried out. This one features hand-lever starting.
Right Once again, the front forks are Brough's leading-link Castle pattern. The fuel tank includes a tool cupboard on its underside.
Far right The Dream conception was virtually a pair of flat-twins, geared together, with shaft final drive.
Below First machine ever to feature a metallic gold paint scheme, this particular flat-four Brough Superior Dream was the star of the 1938 Earls Court Show, but failed to reach production.

1954 646 cc BSA A10 Golden Flash

Following the trend set by Triumph in immediate pre-war days, BSA entered the vertical-twin world as soon as possible after the return of peace, initially with a 495 cc twin from the drawing board of Herbert Perkins. This was the original A7, and frankly it was not the unqualified success for which the makers had hoped. True, it had to cope with the execrable 73 octane pool petrol which was all that the government of the day would permit to be sold, but even so, the A7 cylinder head was imperfectly cooled and, in conjunction with a none-too-clever combustion chamber shape, the engine tended to overheat and run on, even with the ignition switched off.

To rectify matters, BSA recruited Bert Hopwood from Norton Motors (where he had designed the first Norton Dominator vertical twin), and Bert's first job on joining Small Heath in May 1949, was to redesign the A7 (but discreetly, leaving the general appearance unchanged so far as possible). This he did, altering the bore and stroke and designing a cylinder head with much improved cooling and a far better combustion chamber. At the same time, however, he evolved a 646 cc unit which made use of as many of the smaller twin's component as was practical.

The newcomer was announced as the Model A10 in October 1949, when it was offered with a choice of rigid frame or plunger rear springing. At that time, it was stated in the press that 'a colour scheme for the new model had yet to be decided upon', but when the doors of the Earl's Court Show opened a month later, we had the answer.

On the plinth stood a machine in perhaps the most handsome finish of any BSA so far produced — a chromium-plated tank with top and side panels in polychromatic golden beige, lined out in maroon. Moreover, the golden beige was not just on the tank but *everywhere*! The A10 had gained a very appropriate name, too — the Golden Flash.

One novelty was that for the first time here was a machine without that pedestrian danger, the registration number plate blade.

Instead, the front mudguard was so deeply valanced that the registration numbers could be painted on the sides of the valances.

For the more sober-sided customer, the A10 could be supplied in black instead of gold, though even in black it retained the Golden Flash name. For several years to come, the A10 would be the mainstay of BSA's vertical-twin range though, inevitably, annual changes were made. The example seen here dates from 1954, by which time the original plunger rear springing had been supplanted by swinging-arm suspension with hydraulic damper units, and a dual seat replaced the single saddle. Current fashion dictated that the headlamp should be housed within a pressed-steel cowl, and the style of painting of the tank had been modified to give chromed side panels.

For the sidecar man, a version with plunger springing, and with the gearbox bolted to the rear of the crankcase to afford semi-unit-construction was available. It was a sign of the times, too, that the black finish was listed as the norm, with golden beige a £3 optional extra. Interestingly, a special version of the A10 was developed for the USA market, with high-compression pistons, Amal TT carburettor, and engine mods which pushed the output to 42 bhp at 6,000 rpm. In fact this was the forerunner of the Rocket series which culminated, in the early 1960s, in the Rocket Gold Star.

Specification

Make BSA. **Model** A10 Golden Flash. **Engine** 646 cc (70 × 84 mm bore and stroke) overhead-valve vertical twin. **Tyres** 3.25 × 19 in front, 3.50 × 19 in rear. **Frame** All-welded duplex tubular cradle with swinging-arm rear springing, hydraulically damped. **Front forks** Hydraulically-damped telescopic. **Brakes** Drums, 8 in diameter front, 7 in diameter rear. **Weight** 408 lb. **Wheelbase** 55 in. **Manufacturer** BSA Motor Cycles Ltd, Armoury Road, Small Heath, Birmingham.

Above Use of an all-over finish of pale golden beige was, in the eyes of many BSA enthusiasts, a touch of sheer genius, producing the most handsome BSA of all.

Right The valanced front mudguard avoided the need for a separate (and potentially dangerous) front registration plate.

Far right The engine was the work of Bert Hopwood, though based on an earlier Bert Perkins design. A single camshaft is at the rear of the cylinder block.

Below In conjunction with a sprung single saddle, plunger rear suspension gave a reasonably comfortable ride. Magneto and dynamo are separate instruments.

1963 646 cc BSA Rocket Gold Star

Most glamorous of all the pre-unit BSA vertical twins — that is, those with separate engine and gearbox — the Rocket Gold Star came right at the very end of the A10-type engine's production span. Indeed, the A10 itself had been superseded by the unit-construction A65 when, for the 1962 season, the 'Rocket Goldie' was announced.

The cynics said it was just a way of using up surplus A10 engines, which may have been so, for the 'Rocket Goldie' was only to be manufactured in 1962 and 1963. Yet in that short spell it achieved quite a reputation for itself among the café-racer crowd. In essence, it housed the A10 Super Rocket engine in the duplex-loop Gold Star frame (except that the lower right-hand tube of the frame did not feature the famous kink necessary to give clearance for the Gold Star single's oil pump housing), and to justify the model's name it was given the same finish as the Gold Star — chromium-plated mudguards, chromed tank with silver top panel edged in red and with the circular Gold Star badge in Perspex.

Nor was it all for show, as the engine was equipped with a light-alloy cylinder head offering a 9 to 1 compression ratio, and sports camshafts, plus a racing-style magneto with manual advance and retard control. The exhaust system was 'Siamesed' and, on the right, linked to a single silencer of the Gold Star's 'twittering' type. Matched speedometer and rev-counter were mounted on the front fork top yoke, and a lengthy list of optional equipment included light-alloy wheel rims, track silencer, a 190 mm front brake in a full-width hub, a close-ratio gearbox, and a five-gallon racing tank in light alloy.

Power output was a healthy 46 bhp at 6,250 rpm, though this could be pushed up to 50 bhp with the track silencer. The machine could have made a useful clubman racing model, though perhaps it had come on the scene a little too late for that. Nevertheless, *The Motor Cycle* road-tested a Rocket Goldie in its standard steel-rim form in November 1962 and gave it a really glowing report.

Headlining it as a 'scintillating high-performance road-burner', the magazine wrote about the effortless, surging acceleration through the gears and a tireless 90 mph cruising speed. 'The maximum of 105 mph obtained on test,' commented tester David Dixon, 'could certainly have been bettered had the November weather been co-operative.' David was, however, rather critical of the handling, for though it was precise up to 90 mph, it then became progressively lighter until, at 105 mph on a wet road, the front wheel tended to wander slightly. Stiffening the action of the front fork would probably, he suggested, eliminate the tendency for rolling on fast corners. 'It was,' he concluded, 'that rare bird, a high-performance motorway express which is almost equally at home in less exciting urban surroundings.'

Yet the Rocket Goldie did have a chance or two to share racing glory, especially in the Thruxton 500-Miler of 1963 when Ron Langston and Dave Williams shared the saddle of one. Indeed, they had worked up into an encouraging third place overall, with prospects of going higher, but only to drop back down the field after an oil union broke.

With the announcement in October 1963 of the new season's range, the Rocket Gold Star had gone, and in its place was a Rocket version of the unit-construction A65. Yet there *was* a new Rocket Goldie on the market, and at a cost of only 5s 6d (27½p); the price was the clue, for it was a plastic model kit, from Revells!

Specification

Make BSA. **Model** Rocket Gold Star. **Engine** 646 cc (70 × 84 mm bore and stroke) overhead-valve vertical twin. **Tyres** 3.25 × 19 in front, 3.50 × 19 in rear. **Frame** All-welded duplex tubular cradle with swinging-arm rear suspension, hydraulically damped. **Front forks** Hydraulically damped telescopic. **Brakes** Drums, 8 in diameter front, 7 in diameter rear. **Weight** 418 lb. **Wheelbase** 55 in. **Manufacturer** BSA Motor Cycles Ltd, Armoury Road, Small Heath, Birmingham.

Above Lashings of chromium plating, a deep tank with 'Goldie' top panel in frosted silver...no wonder it was the darling of café-racer society!

Right The 190 mm racing front brake is directly derived from Gold Star racing practice.

Far right Last of BSA's pre-unit-construction twins, the Super Rocket engine offered high compression pistons, a sports camshaft and die-cast cylinder head.

Below Surely one of the most handsome machines ever to emerge from Small Heath, the coveted 'Rocket Goldie' allied the Super Rocket engine with the much-respected Gold Star frame.

1971 654 cc BSA A65FS Firebird Scrambler

What on earth is a Firebird, and whoever heard of a 654 cc vertical-twin scrambler? Perhaps nobody this side of the Atlantic Ocean, but the Firebird was a version of the high-performing BSA Lightning twin produced especially for the American market, where the term 'scrambler' has a rather different connotation. We tend to think of a scrambles machine as a purpose-built motocross model, but to the American enthusiast it is a road-legal device with a macho image, capable of being ridden across open desert when the opportunity presents itself.

Earlier in this book we studied two presentations of the pre-unit-construction 646 cc BSA twin, but from 1962 onwards this was superseded by a very neat unit-construction motor known as the A65 — an engine, by the way, which was to earn a very good name for itself in sidecar road-racing in the hands of such exponents as Mick Boddice, Chris Vincent, Peter Brown and Roy Hanks.

For a number of years, the standard A65 had an appreciative British following, but with the factory tending to concentrate on the wishes of the American market, the specification began to grow more and more outlandish, and the long-suffering British had to put up with skimpy mudguards (does it *never* rain in California?), high handlebars, small-capacity fuel tanks, a headlamp carried on bent wire instead of proper brackets and other similar fancies.

The ultimate inanity was the oil-carrying frame introduced for 1971, based on a large-diameter backbone from which depended duplex cradle loops. The dual seat was easily 2 in too high off the ground; testers told the management that, and so did unfortunate journalists who tried out the prototypes, but it was like beating one's head against a brick wall. The frame was put into production, not only for BSA but also for Triumph twins. The Triumph people brought down the seat height, but BSA never did and this must surely have played a major part in the fast-approaching downfall of the factory.

As for the Firebird Scrambler, that had originally come into the range in 1968, using the then-conventional frame to meet American demands for a super-powerful on-or-off-the-road machine. Essentially it was a Lightning, with the power output raised to 54 bhp, and in the 1971 guise as seen here it had the usual high-rise handlebars, twin high-level exhaust pipes on the left (painted matt black and given the dubious protection of a skimpy-looking wire mesh guard), and a 'bash plate' bolted to the lower run tubes of the frame to protect the underside of the crankcase from rocky contact.

With the introduction of the new frame came front forks without gaiters or shrouds, the chromium-plated stanchion tubes being subjected to all the grit that was flying around. The wheel spindle was secured to the base of the cast-light-alloy sliders by caps held by four studs. Conical light-alloy wheel hubs were featured front and rear, and the front brake was a twin-leading-shoe design.

The Firebird Scrambler was produced in this guise for just one year, because BSA were now travelling faster and faster down the slippery slide to oblivion. A brief programme was announced for 1972, embracing the Lightning and Thunderbolt twins, backed by a 500 cc single and the three-cylinder Rocket 3, but the Firebird had flown, and in any case, BSA production did not last to the end of the 1972 season.

Specification

Make BSA. **Model** A65FS Firebird Scrambler.
Engine 654 cc (75 × 74 mm bore and stroke) overhead-valve vertical twin.
Tyres 3.50 × 19 in front, 4.00 × 18 in rear.
Frame All-welded duplex tubular loop, with large-diameter oil-carrying top tube and swinging-arm rear springing.
Front forks Telescopic, hydraulically damped.
Brakes Drum, 8 in diameter twin-leading-shoe front, 7 in diameter rear. **Weight** 411 lb.
Wheelbase 54¼ in. **Manufacturer** BSA Motor Cycles Ltd, Armoury Road, Small Heath, Birmingham.

Above Skimpy front guard, and 'Star Wars' exhaust layout showed just how far out of touch with reality BSA designers had grown in the final phase.
Right One of the few good points of the design was the conical front hub.
Far right Engine unit is essentially the A65 twin but with a boosted power output. The Firebird Scrambler came almost at the end of BSA production.
Below Not a scrambler in British terms — that's what the Americans called it. But the big drawback was that it was 2 in too high for the average rider.

1914 744 cc Clyno 5-6 hp

The Clyno is one of Britain's long-forgotten makes, and yet there was a time when it was one of the best-known, with a very important part to play during the First World War. So when and why did it fade out? The story reflects the ambitions of one man — Frank Smith, of Thrapston in Northamptonshire — to become a motor magnate, by directly challenging people like William Morris and Herbert Austin in the popular car market. The Clyno car was (initially, anyway) a good one, but in Smith's efforts to undercut Morris and Austin prices, the quality was gradually cut until Clyno went to the wall in 1928, unable to stand the heat of the battle.

In the beginning, though, Frank Smith and his cousin Alwyn were accessory manufacturers, patenting and producing such items as an engine-shaft adjustable pulley with which a rider could alter the ratio of his single-speed machine, by closing or opening the pulley flanges, and a bolt-on prop stand. But in 1909 Clyno entered the motorcycle market, with a 3 hp single and a 6 hp vee-twin, both powered by engines supplied by the Stevens Motor Manufacturing Company.

It was about the same time, that the Stevens brothers were themselves thinking of going into motorcycle making, and the first AJS made its appearance in the ACU Quarterly Trials of August 1910. By an odd coincidence, Frank and Alwyn Smith, on Stevens-powered Clyno twins, were both entered for the same event. Be that as it may, the Stevens family were more than pleased with the behaviour of their prototype, and decided to go into production with it at a new works in Wolverhampton. That meant that they would no longer be able to supply engines to Clyno, but it was suggested that Clyno could take over and manufacture the Stevens vee-twin engine under their own name, and since the old Stevens factory would be vacant, they could move from Thrapston and take over that as well.

That seemed a good idea all round, and in the next few years the Clyno twin (the four-stroke single was dropped) advanced considerably. Designer William Comery joined them in 1913, and his work included enlarging the engine from 644 to 744 cc, and evolving a massive three-speed countershaft gearbox to replace the earlier two-rear-chain gearing system. He gave the twin quickly-detachable and interchangeable wheels, and handsome cast-light-alloy primary and secondary chaincases, and as a second-string model, designed a very neat little unit-construction 269 cc Clyno two-stroke.

The 1914 744 cc Clyno twin came at just the right time, for it proved to be the ideal bike for the machine-gun sidecar outfits that would be used in considerable numbers by the British Army in the First World War. There were other makes — some batteries were issued with Scott outfits, others had Royal Enfields — but the Clyno was the most numerous and gave sterling service on the battlefields. After the war, the company returned to the motorcycle market for a few years, but Frank Smith was determined to move to four wheels, to which end the company underwent financial reconstruction in 1922. It was, alas, a fatal move and results were to show that he would have done far better had he stuck to bikes! The trouble was that the Pelham Street works and the new factory at Bushbury to which he moved later just did not have the resources for mass production of cheap cars.

Specification

Make Clyno. **Model** 5-6 hp. **Engine** 744 cc (76 × 82 mm bore and stroke) side-valve 55° vee-twin. **Tyres** 26 × 3 in beaded edge front and rear. **Frame** Brazed-lug tubular diamond. **Front forks** Druid side-spring girders. **Brakes** Stirrup-type front brake, 6 in diameter drum rear. **Weight** 265 lb. **Wheelbase** 59 in. **Manufacturer** Clyno Manufacturing Co Ltd, Pelham Street, Wolverhampton.

Above The Clyno was noted for the superb quality of the cast light-alloy employed throughout; this included the chaincases.

Right For a powerful vee-twin, use of a bicycle-type stirrup front brake was somewhat archaic. Druid forks were soon to be replaced by Brampton Biflex.

Far right Earlier Clyno twins employed an engine of Stevens design and make, from which William Comery developed the 1914 744 cc model.

Below A finish of French grey and dark blue made the big Clyno look almost dainty — but there was nothing dainty about its wartime performance as a machine-gun haulier.

1928 980 cc Coventry-Eagle Flying Eight

With a rounded and tapered fuel tank, and an exciting-looking 980 cc vee-twin JAP power unit, Coventry-Eagle's famous Flying Eight bears a striking resemblance to a Brough-Superior of the same period. That is not really surprising, for George Brough and Percy Mayo of the Coventry-Eagle company spent some time together towards the end of the First World War discussing the type of motorcycle they would like to manufacture when the hostilities were over, and they found their tastes were remarkably similar.

There had been a JAP-engined vee-twin in the Coventry-Eagle range for a couple of years before the announcement of the first Flying Eight in March 1923, but the new model was one, reported *The Motor Cycle*, 'which should make a special appeal to speedmen'. So it should, indeed, for it was powered by a special 976 cc side-valve engine which gave the machine a guaranteed 80 mph maximum speed — not at all bad for a side-valve.

The model was continued virtually unchanged until the 1926 season when a new overhead-valve version of the Flying Eight appeared in the catalogue. This one again used a JAP power unit, but of 980 cc and driving through a Nottingham-built Jardine gearbox. Other features were heavy-duty Webb girder front forks, and 8 in diameter Royal Enfield brakes on both wheels. The improved side-valve model, meanwhile continued in production alongside.

Although the 1930s found Coventry-Eagle as producers of ride-to-work models by the thousand (in 1932, their total output even exceeded that of BSA, though that was somewhat exceptional), they did acquire quite a respectable racing record in the 1920s, notably with Bert Le Vack, Teddy Prestwich and Percy Brewster breaking records on JAP-engined singles of 250 and 350 cc. But the big Flying Eight was by no means overlooked, and in 1925 H. Harte and Stan Glanfield shared a 980 cc outfit to break a whole hatful of records from four to nine hours in Class G (1,000 cc sidecars) at speeds from 65 to 67 mph.

Even greater glory was to come in November of 1928 when, just before the Brooklands track closed for the winter, one-legged Harold Taylor took out a Flying Eight outfit for an all-out attack on the Class G 200 mile record. Harold (in post-war years the manager of Britain's Grand Prix des Nations moto-cross team) did the job handsomely, setting up a speed of 80.79 mph. The outfit on which the record was made is now in the hands of a Vintage MCC enthusiast.

By 1928, the year of manufacture of the National Motorcycle Museum's Flying Eight, the machine had acquired Magdyno electric lighting, Ghost silencers, and a steering damper. By any standards it was a most imposing machine, but the Coventry-Eagle company was changing direction and from now on the main emphasis would be on the unusual pressed-steel frame lightweights rather than the big-twins. The last ohv Flying Eight was made in 1930, with the side-valve model surviving for only one season more before it, too was axed. Not even the four-cam side-valve Police model tempted many customers, it seemed.

As Britain recovered from the slump of the early 'thirties, so Coventry-Eagle reintroduced a 'Flying' range of sportsters, but this time they were singles, using Matchless engines, and the twins had gone.

Specification

Make Coventry-Eagle. **Model** Flying Eight. **Engine** 980 cc (85.7 × 85 mm bore and stroke) JAP 50-degree overhead-valve vee twin. **Tyres** 3.25 × 19 in front and rear. **Frame** Brazed-lug tubular cradle, unsprung at rear. **Front forks** Webb girders. **Brakes** 8 in diameter drums front and rear. **Weight** 395 lb. **Wheelbase** 59 in. **Manufacturer** Coventry Eagle Cycle and Motor Co Ltd, Bishopsgate Green Works, Coventry.

Above There are many similarities between the Coventry-Eagle twin and the Brough Superior, which were both aimed at the big sports-roadster market.
Right By 1928, the big-twin market was shrinking, and Coventry-Eagle were about to go whole-heartedly for utility two-strokes.
Far right Like Brough, the Coventry factory employed 998 cc JAP engines, in both side-valve or (as here) overhead-valve form. The hand-operated oil pump on the tank top is untidy.
Below Nice touch — the rear of the fuel tank is protected by a leather wrapping.

1981 992 cc Hesketh V1000

No new make of motorcycle could ever have been launched on such a flood-tide of good wishes as the big vee-twin Hesketh. All of Britain's old-established factories had already gone to the wall, and yet here was a total newcomer of imposing appearance, aimed at the very top end of the market; a Bentley among motorcycles built by a company fronted by no less a personage than Lord Thomas Alexander Fermor Hesketh, who had earlier sponsored a Formula One car road-racing team (remember the teddy-bear mascot?) with James Hunt as the Number One driver.

Enthusiasts everywhere were *willing* the new Hesketh bike to be a success and, when shares in Hesketh Motor Cycles plc were floated, plenty of ordinary motorcyclists bought a few, just to show they had faith in British industry. The new machine was given its official launch in April 1980 in a marquee in the grounds of Lord Hesketh's stately home, Easton Neston, by Towcester racecourse. Indeed, the prototype models had been built in the stable block of Easton Neston House, where quite sophisticated plant had been installed in car racing days.

Production, however, was to take place at a factory on a Daventry industrial estate, though it would be over two years before the Daventry plant was officially opened. The trouble was that press tests of the prototype models had shown up some serious faults, in particular a clumsy and far from reliable gear change, and excessive mechanical noise. It was largely a matter of 'back to the drawing board', but while the transmission was being revamped and other faults put right, no bikes were leaving the end of the assembly track and no cash was coming in.

By September of 1981 there was disturbing news from the City of London, where the value of Hesketh shares on the Stock Exchange had dropped sharply. A restart of production was planned for Christmas — and progressively delayed until the first of the redesigned bikes began to roll out of the works in February 1982. Two months later, Hesketh took stand space at the Motor Cycle Show at Birmingham's NEC, and announced that the selling price was now only £5 short of a shattering £5,000!

But by June the adventure was over. Trading in Hesketh shares had been suspended and the company was bankrupt. After a struggle to complete work in hand with a caretaker staff, the operation was shut down in August, and the entire contents of the Daventry works — including 30 bikes, some of them 'Show only' and probably without internals — was put up for auction. Only 139 Hesketh V1000 twins had been built.

Yet it was not the end, after all, and with the setting up of a new company, jigs and tools were acquired from the receiver. Production restarted on a much smaller scale at Easton Neston, the occasional bike being assembled now and again, and about 40 more Heskeths had been built until in 1985 the venture shut down again — with hints that it might not be the finish, even now, as London dealers Mocheck were showing interest.

Totally unlike any bike built in Britain before, the Hesketh was huge and heavy, akin to some of the Japanese monsters. It could have succeeded if established motorcycle men been heading the company. But then again — established motorcycle men would never have built a bike like the Hesketh V1000!

Specification

Make Hesketh. **Model** V1000. **Engine** 992 cc (95 × 70 mm bore and stroke) four-valve, double-overhead-camshaft 90° vee-twin. **Tyres** 4.10V18 front, 5.10V17 rear. **Frame** All-welded tubular 'space frame' with engine forming stressed lower member. Swinging-arm rear suspension, hydraulically damped. **Front forks** Hydraulically damped telescopic. **Brakes** Twin discs at front, single disc at rear. **Weight** 506 lb. **Wheelbase** 59½ in. **Manufacturer** Hesketh Motor Cycles plc, Daventry, Northants.

Above Only 139 Hesketh V1000s were built before the Daventry venture went into liquidation.

Right Note the plate-light-alloy construction of the wheels. Twin discs help to halt the front wheel.

Far right A double-overhead-camshaft 90° vee-twin served as a stressed member of the frame assembly.

Below Up-to-the-minute styling took the Hesketh firmly into the 1980s, but the imposing heavyweight was let down by its mechanical design.

1939 592 cc Levis 600

The last Levis motorcycles were built in 1939, production ceasing on the outbreak of war. However, the company is still in existence at the familiar old address at Stechford, Birmingham. Today they add an extra 's' to the name, and are known as Leviss Ltd to avoid confusion with the clothing manufacturer and to emphasise to their Middle Eastern customers that they have no Israeli connection. (In fact, the Levis name comes from the Latin, the company's motto being *Levis et Celer*, 'Light and Swift'.)

To vintage enthusiasts, the Levis name is inevitably associated with a series of very sturdy and very efficient two-strokes (they won the 1922 Lightweight TT with one) but from the later 'twenties onward the makers the Butterfield brothers moved more and more into the field of four-strokes, starting with a 350 cc, the 'A Special'. Gradually the range was enlarged to embrace the 'B Special' 250, and 'D Special' 500 but, oddly enough, the 592 cc model introduced for the 1937 season never had any particular catalogue designation and was always just the '600'.

The first Levis four-strokes used a traditional diamond-type frame with the engine crankcase forming the lower section, but with the new '600' there came the first Levis cradle frame, with a tapering-tube front down member extended to meet twin lower cradle stays passing under the engine to a large lug beneath the gearbox.

Engine design was also improved over earlier overhead-valve Levis models, with a cleaned-up crankcase assembly in which internal strengthening ribs were substituted for the early-pattern external ribs. Tappets were dispensed with, and instead the lower ends of the pushrods bore directly on the cam followers. The pushrods were encased in a chromium-plated tube which gave the engine something of the appearance of an overhead-camshaft design. For the first time in Levis history, the valves and rocker gear were enclosed, and were lubricated from the externally-mounted Pilgrim pump.

The Burman four-speed gearbox was of-fered with a choice of high or low ratios. There was the option of either Druid or Webb front forks as preferred. Electrics were supplied by a Miller Dynomag, and the headlamp was an impressive 8 in diameter. An upswept exhaust pipe was standard — and the works catalogue code for the model was 'Cool'!

At a dry weight of 375 lb, the '600' was quite heavy by the standards of the time, a problem not helped by the use of a molybdenum-alloy cast-iron barrel and head but that didn't deter Bob Foster. Best known as a road-racer, of course, Bob was in fact an all-rounder, and he used a specially-prepared '600' with great gusto in both scrambles and hill-climbs — and those who can recall seeing him in action on the big Levis will testify that Bob's nickname of 'Fearless Foster' was well-merited!

Almost equally intrepid was well-known trials rider Henry Laird who, as Midland Editor of *Motor Cycling*, road-tested a Levis 600 in June, 1938. 'The most outstanding qualities of this large single-cylinder,' he wrote, 'were the beefy power and the delightfully smooth way in which it was delivered. In addition, the economical running was more in keeping with a three-fifty instead of a machine of nearly twice that capacity'. In fact, 90 mph and 80 mpg; pretty good, wouldn't you agree?

Specification

Make Levis. **Model** Model 600.
Engine 592 cc (82 × 112 mm bore and stroke) overhead-valve single. **Tyres** 3.00 × 21 in front 4.00 × 19 in rear. **Frame** Brazed-lug tubular cradle. No rear springing. **Front forks** Webb girders. **Brakes** Drums, 7 in diameter front, 8 in diameter rear. **Weight** 375 lb. **Wheelbase** 55 in. **Manufacturer** Butterfields Ltd, Old Station Road, Stechford, Birmingham.

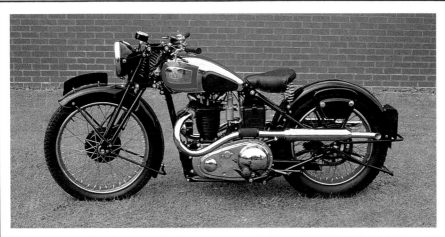

Above Far removed from the Levis company's vintage image as makers of small two-strokes, the 1939 '600' was a rugged and very sporty machine.
Right Essentially a roadster, the Levis '600' had a fine off-road record in the hands of Bob Foster. The manufacturers now make air compressors.
Far right Total valve-gear enclosure, and twin high-level exhaust pipes were modern features for the time — but lubrication was still total-loss.
Below Never one of Britain's really big factories, Levis concentrated on high quality, of which this is a superb example.

1923 678 cc Martinsyde Six

The trouble with being involved in the supply of arms and equipment during a major war is that when the shooting stops, so does the lucrative flow of military contracts. The supplier is left with an empty, echoing factory while he searches frantically for some alternative and peaceable product with which to fill it. Several firms found themselves in this position following the signing of the Armistice in November 1918, and one such was Martin and Handasyde of Woking, who had been producing Martinsyde fighters for the RAF and its predecessor, the Royal Flying Corps.

Late in 1919 came the announcement of a new motorcycle, to be known as the Martinsyde-Newman, a 678 cc 50° vee-twin with the unusual valve arrangement of exhaust-over-inlet, the engine designer being Howard Newman, of the Ivy company, himself a Brooklands racer of considerable repute. 'This machine starts with every hope of success,' said *The Motor Cycle*, in announcing the new model, for it was 'designed by a well-known motorcyclist in conjunction with the experts of an equally well-known aeroplane works with excellent facilities for production'. Production was due to start in January 1920, and the machine would be sold as a complete sidecar outfit, using a handsome coachbuilt body built in Martinsyde's joinery section. To cut corners and put the machine into production quickly, the makers did not design their own gearbox, but opted for the proven AJS box, built in the Woking works under licence.

The 'Newman' part of the name was soon dropped as Martinsyde got into their stride, and for the 1921 season the programme was enlarged by the addition of a sidecar taxi and a light delivery outfit, using the 678 cc power unit, backed by a new 497 cc vee-twin using the same exhaust-over-inlet valve layout. Early Martinsydes used a not particularly distinguished flat-sided fuel tank, but for 1922, as part of a general redesign, the make adopted the cylindrical fuel tank which was to become something of a trade mark for the firm.

The engines remained much as before, but other improvements included a cast-light-alloy primary chaincase, interchangeable wheels and dummy-belt-rim brakes instead of the earlier contracting band and stirrup types. The sidecar outfit was now a particularly handsome tourer, still with Martinsyde's own body, but mounted on a specially-built Mills & Fulford chassis.

One of the best-known Martinsyde models of all joined the range that May. Designed by Harold Bowen (who would later join Amal carburettors), it was the 739 cc Quick Six, a solo sports twin; and there was another new model to come — a 346 cc single, still with exhaust-over-inlet engine, which took the Martinsyde company into the smaller-capacity market for the first time.

The 1922 Martinsydes represented the make in full flowering, and the all-round sturdiness of that year's models was such that one of them — a 1922 678 cc Six, ridden solo — made headlines 62 years later, when it carried Neil Bromilow on a round-Australia tour of just under 10,000 miles over largely indifferent roads and tracks.

Sadly, though, time was fast running out for the Martinsyde company, and production ended mid-way through 1923, the jigs, tools, and goodwill being sold that October to the older-established Bat firm. For a short while the twin came back, now labelled the Bat-Martinsyde, but the venture did not last. Nevertheless, the old factory at Woking was to retain a motorcycle connection for many years to come, because the new occupiers made gasket material.

Specification

Make Martinsyde. **Model** 6 hp. **Engine** 678 cc (70 × 88 mm bore and stroke) exhaust-over-inlet 50° vee-twin. **Tyres** 26 × 3.00 in beaded-edge. **Frame** Brazed-lug tubular diamond, unsprung at rear. **Front forks** Brampton Biflex girders. **Brakes** Dummy vee-belt rim, front and rear. **Weight** (solo) 280 lb. **Wheelbase** 57 in. **Manufacturer** Martinsyde Ltd, Maybury Hill, Woking, Surrey.

Above The joinery section of the Martinsyde works produced the touring sidecar.

Right Brampton Biflex front forks were so named because they were sprung both vertically and fore-and-aft.

Far right Securing the cylindrical fuel tank by nickel-plated bands was also done by NUT.

Below There were a number of unusual features, including exhaust-over-inlet valve arrangement.

1933 592 cc Matchless Model B Silver Hawk

What a fascinating display must have met the eyes of the visitor to the Olympia Motor Cycle Show in November 1930. Virtually every manufacturer had something new and exciting (New Hudson, for example, had completely revamped their range from head to toe), and there was not just *one* totally new British four-cylinder to be seen, but *two*! We met one of the new 'fours' earlier in this book, in the shape of the Ariel Square Four. Now meet its rival, the Matchless Silver Hawk which was, or so the makers claimed in their sales literature, 'unquestionably the most fascinating machine to ride that has ever been built. It combines the silence, smoothness and comfort of the most expensive motor car with a super-sports performance. On top gear alone the machine will run from as low as 6 miles per hour to over 80 miles per hour, while the acceleration given by the four-cylinder overhead-camshaft engine in conjunction with the four-speed gearbox must be experienced to be believed.'

That says it all, really. But for all its proclaimed virtues, the Matchless Four did not exactly take the world by storm, and after struggling on for a few seasons, it was quietly dropped from the range in 1935. No discredit to the bike itself, of course, but these were the Hungry 'Thirties, the years of the Great Depression and the money was scarce. There was possibly enough of a market to support one luxury four-cylinder model, but not two. In a head-on battle for sales, the Ariel Square Four won, and the rival Matchless Silver Hawk lost out.

Still, the Hawk was quite an imaginative design, and for all its resemblance to the Square Four it was actually a narrow-angle vee-four much in common with the same factory's Silver Arrow monobloc twin of the previous year. There was just one crankshaft set across the frame and, unusually, it had a centre bearing mounted in a plate — a feature that would be repeated a couple of decades later in the AJS and Matchless vertical twins.

A single overhead camshaft ran across the cylinder head, driven at the right-hand side by a substantial shaft and bevel-gear arrangement. Ignition was by dynamo and coil, the dynamo being driven by skew gearing from the camshaft-drive vertical shaft. The oiling system was dry-sump, with the oil carried in a pressed-steel tank at the base of the front-down tube, bolted directly to the engine's crankcase.

The frame was the one which also housed the smaller vee-twin, and featured cantilever rear springing in which the rear sub-frame pivoted in Silentbloc rubber-bonded bushes behind the gearbox. Two compression springs were mounted under the saddle, and damping was by friction discs, controlled by a knob. Brakes were coupled 8 in diameter, meaning that both front and rear drums came into operation if the brake pedal was pressed, but the handlebar lever operated the front brake alone.

In the years ahead, Matchless carried out very little development on the Silver Hawk, except that in its final period a foot gear-change was available to option at £1 10s extra, and it seemed almost as though they themselves had little faith in it. Perhaps they hadn't: when 'Torrens' of *The Motor Cycle* (editor Arthur B. Bourne) wanted to buy a new Silver Hawk in 1935, the makers advised him to go and buy an Ariel instead. Which he did....

Specification

Make Matchless. **Model** Model B Silver Hawk. **Engine** 592 cc (50.8 × 73.02 mm bore and stroke) overhead-camshaft vee-four. **Tyres** 3.25 × 19 in front and rear (4.00 × 19 in at extra cost) wired-on. **Frame** Brazed-lug tubular construction incorporating cantilever rear suspension. **Front forks** Matchless centre-spring girders. **Brakes** Interconnected 8 in diameter drums, front and rear. **Weight** 380 lb. **Wheelbase** 56 in. **Manufacturer** Matchless Motor Cycles (Colliers) Ltd, 44/45 Plumstead Road, Plumstead, London SE 18.

Above Primary drive was by a duplex chain incorporating a Weller spring-blade tensioner, within a massive cast-alloy casing.
Right This was the first appearance of the soon to be famous chromium-plated 'M' tank emblem; note also the polished edges to the mudguards.
Far right The sophisticated specification embraced a narrow-angle monobloc vee-four with shaft-and-bevel driven overhead camshaft.
Below Unfortunately, the imposing Silver Hawk had to battle for its share of the market against the Ariel Square Four — and lost out.

1936 990 cc Matchless Model X

In the last few years before the outbreak of the Second World War, Brough-Superior had switched from JAP power units, to employ instead the 990 cc Matchless vee-twin — side-valve for the Brough–Superior SS80, overhead-valve for the SS100. Yet the odd thing was that Matchless themselves offered a very pleasant vee-twin tourer, with precisely the same engine as supplied to Brough–Superior and just as well-equipped. It was just that George Brough charged £90 for his SS80, while Matchless, without all the ballyhoo and razzmatazz of Brough salesmanship, listed their Model X at only £69 15s!

In fact the Matchless factory had been noted for big vee-twins since before the First World War, originally with engines by MAG or JAP, but by the mid-'thirties the Model X enjoyed a gently bovine engine designed and built on the Plumstead premises. It was 'designed for the big-twin enthusiast and, of course, with a special eye for heavy-duty sidecar work', to which end the 1936 version had been given more robust rear frame members.

However (as George Brough was aware), there were plenty of enthusiasts around who rather liked the idea of a big 'thousand', ridden solo, so at the end of the 1936 season the Model X was revamped and given the catalogue name of Sports Tourist, with a new shorter-wheelbase frame which put the machine on a par with a 500 cc single, as regards roadholding and steering.

The Motor Cycle road-tested the Model X in May 1937, and commented: 'As soon as the machine is on the move the rider forgets that he is astride a heavyweight machine. The Matchless could be ridden feet-up at speeds well below the register of the speedometer without any juggling with the handlebars. At slightly higher speeds the steering was comfortably light, but even when the machine was being cruised at over 60 mph it did not become so light as to necessitate use of the damper.

The excellent roadholding of the Matchless probably accounted to some extent for the effortless way in which it could be cornered.

The big machine could be laid well over on fast corners without any sign of snaking or wandering. On wet roads the Matchless was perfectly stable. Wet tramlines caused the rider no tremors, and on none of the slippery surfaces encountered was a skid experienced. On particularly greasy surfaces the steering tended to become rather light, but this was more a feeling than a fact, for the model never showed any tendency to get out of control.'

Performance of the 990 cc engine was described as 'delightful', and it would accelerate hard in top gear without any trace of snatch from as low as 20 mph. Not really a speedster — it would not be expected of a side-valve, anyway — it would clock up just over 80 mph, and reach 70 mph from a standing start in a quarter of a mile. Particular note was made of the prop-stand, which flew up immediately the bike was brought back to the vertical, a feature which is now compulsory on bikes sold in the USA.

Understandably, the Model X did not feature in competition work, for that was not its *metier*. Instead, it was a highly comforting machine, with a quiet heartbeat and a gentle loping gait which ate up the miles effortlessly. As the 1937 tester put it, the bike 'comes into that aristocratic class of motorcycles that are riders' mounts'. Hear, hear to that!

Specification

Make Matchless. **Model** Model X. **Engine** 990 cc (85.5 × 85.5 mm bore and stroke) 50° side-valve vee-twin. **Tyres** 3.25 × 19 in front, 4.00 × 19 in rear, wired edge. **Frame** Brazed-lug duplex tubular cradle, unsprung at rear. **Front forks** Central spring girders. **Brakes** Drums, 8 in diameter front and rear. **Wheelbase** 57 in. **Weight** 435 lb. **Manufacturer** Matchless Motor Cycles (Colliers) Ltd, 44/45 Plumstead Road, London SE18.

Above A symphony in black and chrome, the Model X represented Plumstead technology at its pre-war best. Power output could be described as 'gently bovine'.
Right A novel detail — the front brake operating cable is routed through one of the tubes of the girder front forks.
Far right A 990 cc unit with detachable cylinder heads, the big Matchless engine was also employed by Brough-Superior, and by Morgan.
Below Though most big side-valve twins were primarily for sidecar use, the Model X was designed specifically as a sporting solo.

1930 680 cc Montgomery Greyhound

One of the lesser-known of Britain's motorcycle manufacturers, Montgomery's were among the pioneers, having built Fafnir-engined models in the 1900s. But William Montgomery was also interested in the problem of carrying a passenger on a motorcycle, and after early experiments he went into production with a sidecar in 1903 almost coincidentally with Graham Brothers, who are generally credited with the invention.

At that time the Montgomery works were located in Bury St Edmunds, Suffolk, and it was from there that a flat-twin Montgomery was announced in 1913. This made use of the prototype Morton & Weaver (Coventry-Victor) flat-twin engine, an unusual feature of which was that the driving pulley was mounted on the end of the camshaft and so ran at half engine-speed.

Wartime brought a halt to Montgomery's motorcycle (but not sidecar) production, and it was not until 1922 that the company re-entered the two-wheeler field, this time, from works in Coventry.

As befits a sidecar pioneer, Montgomery had two entries in the first Sidecar TT in 1923, one driven by W. Montgomery in person, though sad to say neither outfit finished. Later, though, Montgomery solos were quite regular contestants both at Brooklands and in the Isle of Man, and fourth and sixth places in the 1924 Junior TT can be counted as very respectable performances.

The company also manufactured frames and other components for rival manufacturers, notably Poppe & Packman, and it was a disastrous fire which led to the eventual passing of P & P; the Montgomery works were totally gutted in December 1925, and as a result Montgomery machines were off the market for two years. The P & P concern, less financially well-heeled than Montgomery, was unable to survive the enforced stoppage of production, and sold the business to Wooler.

Once Montgomery were back, they expanded the range considerably so that by 1930 they were able to offer a comprehensive selection of two-strokes, four-strokes, both side-valve and overhead-valve, singles and twins from 250 and 750 cc. Boosted by

the fact that Syd Jackson had won TT replicas in the Lightweight, Junior and Senior races on Montgomery models, the firm announced that 'TT experience has been utilised in the design of all Montgomery frames and forks, and comfortable riding positions with easy steering have been attained'.

Well, perhaps; but the frame lower rear stays seemed to finish a little oddly, beneath the gearbox. The Greyhound models were the top of the range and, not surprisingly, had a standard finish of grey enamel, although for 15s 6d extra the fuel tank and mudguards could be specially finished in red, apple green or ivory.

As the depression years of the early 'thirties began to bite, so Montgomery cut back on their range, and to save expense adopted the practice of channelling their entire output through one London dealer, in this case Renno's of Islington. Yet things did improve, and as Britain started to pull back into prosperity, so Montgomery spread their wings again, announcing for the 1939 season a selection of mounts extending from 98 and 125 cc Villiers lightweights, up to JAP-powered four-strokes in standard and de luxe editions, the latter (250, 350 and 500 cc) featuring new cradle frames incorporating plunger-type rear suspension.

But the clouds were gathering, and with the declaration of war Montgomery production ended. As late as 21 September 1939, Renno's were advertising 'New Machines Actually In Stock for Immediate Delivery', but that was all.

Specification

Make Montgomery. **Model** Greyhound. **Engine** JAP 680 cc (85.5 × 85 mm bore and stroke) overhead-valve 50° vee-twin. **Tyres** 3.50 × 19 in front and rear, wired edge. **Frame** Brazed-lug diamond construction. No rear springing. **Front forks** Brampton girders. **Brakes** Drums, 7 in diameter front and rear. **Weight** 370 lb. **Wheelbase** 56½ in. **Manufacturer** W. Montgomery & Co, Leicester Causeway, Coventry.

Above Although not one of the better-known of British motor cycles, the Coventry-built Montgomery gained quite a faithful following. Production ended at the outbreak of war, and was never resumed.

Right Many makers in the 1930s adopted a policy of channelling their entire output through one dealer; in Montgomery's case, the dealer was Renno's of Islington.

Far right Most Montgomery machines employed JAP power units, and this overhead-valve 680 cc makes an attractive package.

Below Greyhounds are traditionally long and lean...

1964 646 cc Norton Dominator 650SS

It is a sad note in Norton history that the very last motorcycles to be constructed in the firm's traditional home at Bracebridge Street, Aston, Birmingham were a batch of 650SS twins in police trim to the order of the Queensland (Australia) Police. However, it was not the end of the line, for the model survived the trauma of a move to the parent AMC factory at Plumstead and was soon rolling again. The very last 650SS was built in February 1970, having overlapped the later Commando by exactly two years.

Lineal descendant of the first Norton vertical twin (the 497 cc Model 7 Dominator of 1948, a classic design from the drawing board of Bert Hopwood whose later work would include the BSA A10 Golden Flash and — with Doug Hele — the Triumph Trident three-cylinder), the 650 cc Super Sports had entered the Norton range for the 1962 season, and so quickly became a firm favourite with the British motorcycling public that by the end of its first year it was voted 'Machine of the Year', in *Motor Cycle News*'s prestigious competition. Nor was that a flash in the pan, for it came top of the voting in 1963, too, to win the magnificent trophy twice on the trot.

Carrying its engine upright, the 650SS made use of the classic race-proved Norton Featherbed duplex-loop frame with Norton Roadholder telescopic forks at the front. It looked very similar to other Norton twins to the casual glance, but in fact the internals were stiffened up to cope with the extra power, so the built-up crankshaft had larger-diameter big end journal bearings, and a heavier central flywheel. Pistons were solid-skirt, and there was a new type of light-alloy cylinder head with a marked downdraught carburettor intake — a development derived directly from the success of Doug Hele's Domiracer entry in the 1961 Senior TT.

Siamese exhaust pipes were available on request, but the factory recommended separate pipes, which also gave the machine a more balanced appearance. An extra clutch plate was specified, to cope with the power output (49 bhp at 6,800 rpm).

Inevitably, the machine was entered for production-machine racing, and performed well winning the Silverstone 1,000 km race in 1962, and the Thruxton 500 mile marathon in 1962 and 1963.

The weekly magazines were quick to jump at the chance of road-testing the machine, and it was Vic Willoughby who tried out the model for *The Motor Cycle*. 'Approached two miles a minute yet eats out of your hand!', was his enthusiastic headline — and the record showed that he obtained a best-one-way run of 118 mph on a wet and windy February day. Despite the twin-carburettor arrangement, fuel consumption worked out at an eyebrow-raising 81 mpg at 30 mph, rising to no more than 56 mpg at a steady 60 mph. Those more used to bikes of Oriental origin may curl a sceptic lip, but that is the way British bikes were made.

'It is', concluded Vic, 'a 49 bhp roadster whose quietness, smoothness and lack of fuss make speed deceptive; a machine with such superb handling and braking as to make nearly two miles a minute as safe as a stroll in the garden.' Amen to that!

Specification

Make Norton. **Model** 650 Sports Special. **Engine** 646 cc (68 × 89 mm bore and stroke). **Tyres** 3.00 × 19 in front, 3.50 × 19 in rear, wired edge. **Frame** All-welded duplex tubular cradle, with swinging-arm rear suspension, hydraulically damped. **Front forks** Telescopic, hydraulically damped. **Brakes** Drums, 8 in diameter front, 7 in diameter rear. **Weight** 434 lb. **Wheelbase** 55½ in. **Manufacturer** Norton Motors Ltd, 44 Plumstead Road, London SE 18.

Above Twin low-level exhaust pipes give an air of symmetry. Power output is 49 bhp.

Right Though perhaps a little too firm for some tastes, the famed Norton Roadholder front forks afforded impeccable handling.

Far right Twice voted 'Machine of the Year', the 650SS had an excellent record in production-machine racing. Tachometer drive is taken from the front part of the timing case.

Below To some extent the zenith of Norton's featherbed-framed Dominator vertical-twin series, the 650SS was the last design to emerge from the traditional Bracebridge Street factory.

1965 800 cc Norton P10 (Prototype)

The fuel tank has the familiar Norton finish of silver, lined out in black and red, but the P10 is a machine which never saw the traditional Norton home of Bracebridge Street; it never saw production either, though it did undergo considerable road and track testing, and the possibility of manufacturing the model at the former Villiers works at Wolverhampton was certainly discussed.

The 'P10' designation indicates that it was a Plumstead experimental project. The man responsible was actually Charles Udall, the former Velocette designer who had joined Associated Motor Cycles Ltd at their Plumstead premises in 1961. His P10 project started life as a 750 cc parallel twin, but was soon enlarged to 800 cc, with the engine mounted at a forward inclination in a version of the Norton duplex tubular Featherbed frame.

Built with a five-speed gearbox, the P10 was especially notable for the way in which the twin overhead camshafts were driven by a single length of chain which passed through three small-diameter tubes arranged in the form of a triangle. But there was even more chain than at first appeared, for within the massive timing case (the outside of which was decorated with a kind of boomerang-shaped moulding) it ran round a small engine-shaft sprocket, then round a jockey sprocket, and upwards and backwards to the magneto.

The insides of the narrow chain tubes were coated in non-stick PTFE, and each tube was located at each end in O-ring seals. Sprockets at the right-hand end of each cam-shaft were attached by way of a vernier coupling, to permit any necessary fine adjustment to the timing. In contrast to the massive timing-case cover casting, the primary chaincase cover was just a chromium-plated steel pressing. The rear chain was fully enclosed.

On test, the P10 prototype vibrated rather badly, so AMC development engineer Wally Wyatt tried the effect of fitting rubber bushes to the engine mountings. This was only partially successful, because the swinging arm rear suspension fork was attached to the frame, and when the engine came under load, distortion in its mounting bushes tended to throw the rear chain off its sprockets. However, the germ of an idea was there.

Meanwhile, the AMC combine had suffered financial collapse, and was taken over by Dennis Poore's company under the new title of Norton Villiers Ltd. The main object now was to put a new bike on the market, and after studying the P10 in detail it was decided that a total redesign was necessary, under another code-name — this time Z26. Chain-driven overhead camshafts were to be retained, but the chain now ran from a countershaft at the rear of the cylinder block, and passed upward between the cylinders.

The duplex frame was discarded, and instead a new frame with a large-diameter backbone was substituted. But it was becoming obvious that time was against the team, and that the Z26 would never be tooled up in readiness for the November 1967 deadline set by Dennis Poore. Instead, a new beginning was made, retaining some aspects of the Z26 (the backbone frame, for instance) but using a 750 cc Norton Atlas engine tilted forward, and with the engine, gearbox and rear fork as a sub-unit rubber-mounted from the main frame. Behold — the Commando!

Specification

Make Norton. **Model** P10. **Engine** 800 cc (bore and stroke not disclosed) double-overhead-camshaft parallel twin. **Tyres** 3.25 × 19 in front, 3.50 × 19 in rear, wired edge. **Frame** All-welded duplex tubular loop, swinging-arm rear suspension, hydraulically damped. **Front forks** Telescopic, hydraulically damped. **Brakes** Drums, 8 in diameter front, 7 in diameter rear. **Weight** 405 lb. **Wheelbase** 55½ in. **Manufacturer** Associated Motor Cycles Ltd, 44 Plumstead Road, London SE18.

Above Norton's never produced an overhead-camshaft twin? Oh yes they did — but only one, and this was it!

Right Strictly speaking, the P10 was a Plumstead rather than Norton project, and though it was abandoned some of the development work proved useful for the subsequent Commando.

Far right Chain drive to the overhead camshafts is housed within a triangle of small-diameter cover tubes; still more chain is to be found within the huge timing chest. The prototype covered several thousand miles on road-test.

Below Appearance was quite appealing, but the P10 was heavy and noisy.

1975 850 cc Norton Commando Interstate Mk III

The Norton Commando was launched at the London Show in September of 1967 in 750 cc form, and was largely the responsibility of former Rolls-Royce engineer, Dr Stefan Bauer. In particular, Bauer contributed the backbone frame, with Bernard Hooper and Bob Trigg as the development engineers on the mechanical side.

Because of the deadline imposed by the imminence of the Earl's Court Show, the new Norton Villiers group had taken the 750 cc Norton Atlas parallel twin (itself developed from the earlier Norton Dominator), allied it to an AMC gearbox, and mounted engine and gearbox in a sub-frame isolated from the main duplex tubular frame by a triple arrangement of rubber mountings — above the cylinder head, at the gearbox and in front of the crankcase.

The rear fork was carried on plates from the gearbox, and in this way the engine-gearbox-fork assembly could vibrate as much as it liked without any vibration being transmitted to the main frame and, thereby, to the rider. The system was patented, and was given the name of Isolastic.

Turning to the main frame, the major feature here was the 2¼ in diameter top tube, from which the twin duplex loops descended. As mentioned earlier, the power unit was the Norton Atlas, but it was updated in a number of ways including twin Amal Concentric carburettors, a 12 volt electric supply, triplex primary chain, and a unique diaphragm clutch which afforded above-average grip but which could be lifted when required with a light stroke of the handlebar lever.

Over the years, the Commando would be offered in a variety of styles (Fastback, Hi-Rider, Interstate, etc). It soon became a firm favourite with the British public, and won the 'Machine of the Year' popularity poll conducted by *Motor Cycle News* for an astonishing five years in succession, from 1968 to 1972. Neale Shilton, formerly police-fleet sales manager of Triumph, now joined the group, to develop, demonstrate and sell world-wide a police version of the Commando, known as the Norton Interpol (the Mark I Interpol, of course, for eventually there would be the Wankel-engined Mark II (see page 58)).

From 1973, the original 750 cc Commando was joined by an 850 cc version — strictly speaking an 829 cc — obtained by retaining the original bottom-end assembly and 89 cc stroke, but boring out the barrels from 73 to 77 mm. This was not an unqualified success, however, because the extra power tended to overload the main bearings, a problem not fully overcome until the crankcases were redesigned to incorporate internal strengthening webs.

The machine featured here is the Interstate Mk III, a newcomer for the 1975 season featuring electric starting for the first time. The starter motor is located behind the cylinder block in the position formerly occupied by the magneto, and drives through a train of gears on to a sprag clutch on the engine shaft. New, too, was a change of location of the gear pedal, from right to left to suit USA legislation.

Sadly, Nortons (by this time, Norton Villiers Triumph) again went into liquidation in 1975, the final batch of Commando twins being built in 1978. But the name would live again...

Specification

Make Norton. **Model** Commando Interstate Mk III. **Engine** 829 cc (77 × 89 mm bore and stroke) overhead-valve inclined parallel twin on rubber moutings. **Tyres** 4.10 × 19 in front and rear, wired edge. **Frame** All-welded tubular stucture incorporating duplex loops and large-diameter backbone tube. Swinging-arm rear suspension, hydraulically damped, mounted from gearbox plate. **Front forks** Telescopic, hydraulically damped. **Brakes** Single discs at front and rear. **Weight** 430 lb. **Wheelbase** 57 in. **Manufacturer** Norton Villiers Triumph Ltd, Northway Industrial Estate, Andover, Hants, and Marston Road, Wolverhampton.

Above A 'mile-eater' in the classic British style (despite the left-side gear change pedal, fitted to suit USA legislation).
Right Hydraulically–operated disc brakes are featured at front and rear.
Far right Derivation of the Commando engine from the earlier Dominator design is clear; this one has an electric starter motor behind the cylinder block.
Below After a lapse of several years, Norton's traditional finish of silver tank with red and black pinstriping returned with the Commando Interstate, a machine designed for long-distance fast touring.

1984 588 cc Norton Wankel Interpol Mk II

The Norton Interpol Mk I, a police version of the familiar Commando vertical twin, was developed by Neale Shilton and sold to a large number of police forces world-wide. But the Interpol Mk II was something very different; again a police model, but powered by the unconventional twin-rotor Wankel-type engine with which Nortons (and before them, the BSA group) had been experimenting since the early 1960s.

Originating in Germany, the Wankel principle involved a triangular-shaped rotor revolving inside a semi-oval chamber. Instead of piston rings, there are sealing strips (possibly of ceramic material) at the points of the triangular rotor, and these remain in contact with the chamber walls. As the rotor revolves, so the spaces between the flat sides of the triangle and the chamber walls operate the familiar intake-compression-expansion-exhaust system.

Felix Wankel's conception was acquired by Germany's NSU combine and they, in turn, issued development and manufacturing licences to various other concerns in different countries, for different applications. Japan's Mazda car factory provided perhaps the best-known four-wheel outlet, and from the same country there came the Suzuki RE5 motorcycle — which was scorned by the two-wheel public. In Germany, DKW built the single-rotor Model W2000 motorcycle and achieved modest success, and there were other makers interested, including Rolls-Royce.

In Britain, much of the early development for motorcycle application was undertaken by BSA at their Umberslade Hall research establishment, and the programme was taken up by Norton-Villiers-Triumph after the collapse of the BSA Group. The visible outcome was the Norton Interpol Mk II which began to come into service with Midlands police forces especially, from the early 1980s onward. There was much co-operation between the police and the manufacturers.

Certainly the rotary was fast and exceptionally smooth-running, but a motorcycle-policeman's duties are not confined exclusively to motorway work, and it was in slow-running — for example, when a wide load has to be escorted through a built-up area — that the Interpol found its Achilles' heel. The machine was being built at Norton's Shenstone plant near Lichfield where Doug Hele was brought in as Chief Engineer and, gradually, the snags were ironed out.

'When are we going to have a civilian version?' clamoured potential customers, and the answer was given at the 1987 Motor Cycle Show, where it was announced that just 100 examples of the civilian Norton Classic would be produced. Like the Interpol Mk II, it employed an air-cooled version of the Norton Wankel engine, but the shape of things to come could already be seen on the Norton stand at the show, where a completely redesigned police machine — now named the Commander — was on view. This featured water-cooling, and the implication was that water-cooling would probably be adopted on the civilian model too, once the first 100 were completed.

In a sense, the Norton motorcycle is a means to an end (as is the racing version of the rotary machine), for the company are now deeply involved in building versions of the engine for a variety of purposes, including defence contracts. All the same, keep an eye on your rear-view mirror. That white-fairinged bike sitting on your tail may well have a famous name on its tank.

Specification

Make Norton. **Model** Interpol Mk II. **Engine** 588 cc (nominal) air-cooled twin-rotor Wankel. **Tyres** 100/90V18 front, 110/90V18 rear. **Frame** All-welded tubular, with swinging-arm rear springing, hydraulically damped. **Front forks** Telescopic, hydraulically damped. **Brakes** Twin discs at front, single disc at rear. **Weight** 480 lb. **Wheelbase** 58.5 in. **Manufacturer** Norton Motors Ltd, Lynn Lane, Shenstone, Lichfield, Staffs.

Above The Norton Interpol Mk II was developed for police work.
Right The National Motorcyle Museum exhibit was a police demonstration bike, and has covered many thousands of miles with various forces while on loan.
Far right The power unit is a twin-rotor Wankel-priniciple engine of a nominal 588 cc — air-cooled here, but superseded from 1988 on by a water-cooled engine.
Below Wheels are cast-light-alloy.

1954 598 cc Panther Model 100

People used to speak of the big-single Panther as 'the biggest aspidistra in the world — and all in one pot'; to others, it was 'Big Pussy'. But whatever terms were used, they were always affectionate, for nobody had an unkind word for the Panther. No sportster, it was almost inevitably hitched to a family saloon sidecar, which it hauled without complaint while sipping fuel in a surprisingly abstemious fashion.

Strictly speaking, the Panther name did not come into use until the 1923 season to describe a sports version of the 555 cc side-valve, but the principle of the engine serving in place of the frame down tube went back long before that — to the turn of the century, when Joah Phelon took out patents on the idea. Phelon was in partnership with his nephew Harry Rayner in a small precision wire-drawing business at Cleckheaton near Bradford.

All-chain drive was employed from the start, the first Phelon & Rayner motorcycle being manufactured in March 1901, but the facilities at Cleckheaton allowed for little more than token production, and in December of the same year Phelon allowed the Humber company to build the design under licence, the Coventry-based firm paying a royalty of 7s 6d on each motorcycle produced.

The Humber licence lasted until 1905. Meanwhile, Harry Rayner had been killed in what was reputedly the first car accident in Yorkshire, and from late 1903 Phelon had taken a new partner, Richard Moore. From then on, the Cleckheaton-built machines adopted the P & M trade mark. Moore had himself designed a two-speed gear system involving two primary chains at different ratios, either of which could be chosen through expanding clutches, and this was to be a feature of P & M machines right through to 1922. That included First World War service, where the 499 cc P & M sloper was chosen as the standard wartime mount of the Royal Flying Corps (later, the RAF).

The 598 cc Model 100 Redwing Panther entered the company's range in 1932, and with minimal seasonal modifications it remained in production until as late as 1963. Its 649 cc big sister, the Model 120, outlived it by only three more years. In the 1954 example pictured, we see the Model 100 at its classic best — still Magdyno-equipped, still a twin-port single (a single-port cylinder head could be provided), but with totally-enclosed valve gear and featuring the new P & M-designed telescopic front fork adopted from that year onward. The rigid frame model was available, and many sidecar owners still preferred it, but a swinging-arm rear suspension system was listed for those with more up-to-date ideas.

Indeed, so far round had opinion swung, that after 1957 only the rear-sprung model was manufactured. A P & M sidecar chassis came along in 1957, with non-adjustable arms and intended to be bolted straight on to the Panther's frame, but apart from a few improvements such as full-width wheel hubs and a cush-drive rear hub, development of the Model 100 stagnated during its final few years. The demand for sidecar-hauling motorcycles was dwindling anyway, hit by the advent of the small car, and P & M were running out of cash. Moreover, Burman (the gearbox makers) wanted to concentrate instead on car steering mechanisms for British Leyland, while Lucas gave notice that they were stopping production of the Magdyno. A prototype machine was made with alternator electrics, and an AMC gearbox was tried. But it was too late and the big Panther died in 1966.

Specification

Make Panther. **Model** Model 100.
Engine 598 cc (87 × 100 mm bore and stroke) overhead-valve single. **Tyres** 3.50 × 19 in front and rear, wired edge. **Frame** Brazed-lug tubular, with engine replacing front down tube. No rear suspension.
Front forks Telescopic, hydraulically damped. **Brakes** Drums, 7 in diameter front, 8 in diameter rear. **Weight** 406 lb. **Wheelbase** 55½ in. **Manufacturer** Phelon & Moore Ltd, Horncastle Street, Cleckheaton, Nr Bradford, Yorks.

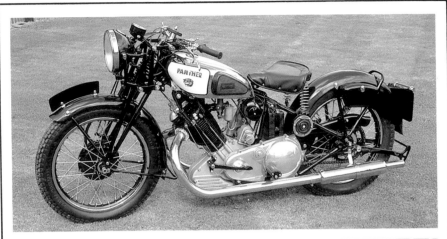

Above Engine is not merely suspended at the cylinder head. Seen here are two of the long bolts which pass around the main bearings and help to support the load.

Right On this pre-war version of the Model 100, the front fork is of girder pattern, but this changed to telescopic on post-war models.

Far right The Model 100 entered the range in 1932 and was continued, with regular improvements, until 1966.

Below Pride of Cleckheaton, the Panther used the engine as part of the frame structure for over 60 years. Primarily, the machine was a sidecar haulier.

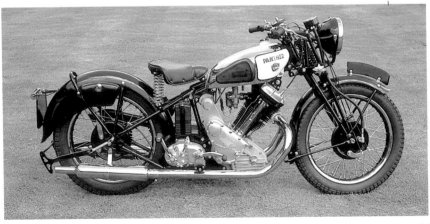

1983 850 cc Quasar Four

Lying well outside the conventional run of motorcycles, the highly futuristic Quasar was the conception of Ken Leaman and Malcolm Newell of Bristol, production being undertaken by Wilson & Sons of that city. From the first machine in 1976 until 1980, only seven machines were sold; manufacture was then taken over by Romarsh Special Products of Calne, Wiltshire and a further ten were built, but Romarsh went into receivership in September of 1982.

But even that was not quite the finish. John Malfoy had been the project manager for the Romarsh company, and he was able to buy sufficient parts from the receiver to permit construction of an additional three models, so bringing the overall Quasar production to just 20. The machine exhibited at the National Motorcycle Museum, and featured on these pages, was the penultimate Quasar ever manufactured, and is a John Malfoy construction.

'The Quasar is the first of a new generation of motorcycles,' stated the maker's promotional literature. 'It is perhaps a startling machine, but if you analyse its concept you will see that it is a natural progression...

'The reclined riding position keeps you comfortable for hours on end, like a quality sports car. The space frame geometry, the fairing, and the long wheelbase give a high-speed stability (and an indifference to crosswinds) that no other motorcycle can compete with...

'The exceptional aerodynamic efficiency makes a positive contribution in the form of supreme road holding, meagre fuel consumption and high top speed (more than 100 mph, carrying two people and luggage). You can cruise at 95 miles per hour all day — and rely on at least 225 miles between fill-ups. And you certainly won't have to give up when the weather's bad!'

But what was that about 'carrying two people'? Surely the Quasar, with its roof and its long, sloping windscreen, is a single-seater? Actually the padded leather strip which affords hammock-type seating is adjustable for position and, when set in its rearmost location, allows two *very* close friends to travel.

The bodywork is of glass fibre, mounted over a duplex tubular space frame which can act also as a rollover bar for crash protection. Perhaps surprisingly, the power unit is the 848 cc light-alloy Reliant water-cooled in-line four, normally to be found in the well-known three-wheeled car, but of course, in a motorcycle of only half the weight of the three-wheeler it can show an impressive turn of speed. The gearbox, too, is Reliant, and there is shaft final drive. Wheels are cast-light-alloy, with twin disc brakes at the front and a single disc at the rear.

A sophisticated specification included twin halogen headlamps, stainless steel fuel tank and exhaust system, two-speed windscreen wiper, an electric starter, and full instrumentation. Quick-release panels provided access to the power unit, and because the weight of the engine and gearbox are carried low, the machine had inherent stability.

A totally practical machine, then, despite its unconventional appearance; but, as the British public have shown so often over the years, unconventionality is *out*. Maybe, some day, somebody will revive the Quasar concept; but not just yet.

Specification

Make Quasar. **Model** 850. **Engine** Reliant 848 cc overhead-valve, water-cooled, light-alloy in-line four-cylinder. **Tyres** 4.25/85H18 tubeless front and rear. **Frame** Duplex tubular all-welded space frame, with swinging-arm rear springing, hydraulically damped. **Front suspension** Pivoted fork, hydraulically damped. **Brakes** Two Lockheed discs at front, single disc at rear. **Weight** 700 lb. **Wheelbase** 77 in. **Manufacturer** Romarsh Special Products, Porte Marsh Road, Calne, Wilts.

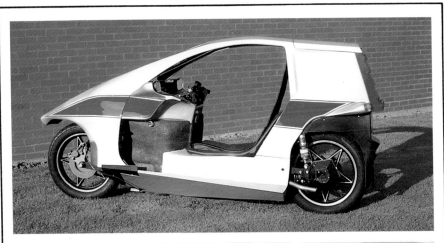

Above The most futuristic motorcycle ever to emerge from a British factory, the Quasar embodied a whole lot of brilliant new ideas.

Right Frontal aspect is slim and wind-cheating. Power unit is a water-cooled four from a Reliant three-wheeler.

Far right The rider adopts a foot-forward position, his back supported by an adjustable hammock strap.

Below Bodywork is of glass-fibre, carried on a duplex tubular space frame which, in an emergency, could provide crash protection.

1921 699 cc Raleigh Model No 9

As mentioned earlier, the man who was principally responsible for the wartime 744 cc Clyno vee-twin, the main transport of Britain's First World War motorized machine gunners, was William Comery, who had joined the Clyno company in 1913. But it should also be said that Comery left Clyno's employment rather abruptly, and by 1917 he was being described as 'chief engineer and works manager of the Raleigh Cycle Co Ltd'. It was also a little suspicious that the swinging-arm rear suspension system which Comery had designed for the proposed post-First World War Clyno should also appear on the flat-twin Raleigh which the Nottingham-based firm first disclosed to the press in May 1918 (at which time it was said that the prototype had been undergoing development testing since April, 1917).

Raleigh had been among the pioneers of Britain's motorcycle industry, but had dropped out in the late 1900s to concentrate on their world-wide bicycle market. That they were considering returning to the powered two-wheel market was a big surprise, and so was the type of machine with which they aimed to make their return. Described as a dual-purpose flat twin, for solo or sidecar work, it was initially an over-square (77 × 70 mm bore and stroke) 654 cc bristling with novelty. Rear springing at this time was rare enough — though Indian had featured it for a couple of years beforehand — but the Comery design actually made use of a strengthened gearbox shell as the pivot point for the swinging-arm. The gearbox was, of course, a Sturmey-Archer, the S-A name being owned by Raleigh anyway.

Other noteworthy features included a special Amac carburettor bolted directly to the timing chest, so that incoming gas received a preliminary warming before passing to the inlet valves, and quickly detachable wheels with knock-out spindles. In the same manner as would be used in later years by several other manufacturers, the rear hub was in two parts, and the wheel could be extracted leaving the rear sprocket and brake drum assembly still in place in the frame. About 75 per cent of the rear mudguard was sprung together with the rear wheel, so that rear tyre clearance remained constant.

But announcing a model is one thing, and putting it into production is another. At the 1920 London Show it was said that 'the first production samples were being exhibited on the Raleigh stand', and *The Motor Cycle*, road-testing the Raleigh twin early in 1921, commented, 'There are few firms capable of retaining interest in a product when more than two years elapse between the lifting of the veil from the first made, and the actual commencement of deliveries. The Raleigh Cycle Company is one of the few.'

In the interval between prototype and production, several changes had been made, most notably that capacity had gone up to 699 cc, and engine dimensions were virtually square rather than over-square. The machine had also gained weight, for though the prototype had weighed only 240 lb, the production version tipped the scales at 290 lb, a hefty 50 lb more. Performance, even solo performance, was disappointing too. 'Fifty-five is claimed by the makers', commented *The Motor Cycle*, 'but in our case we failed to persuade the needle of a reliable speedometer further round the dial than 52 mph.' Oh dear!

But what in fact killed off the Raleigh flat-twin was the cost of production. Although the firm persisted for a few seasons, from 1924 onward the machine was replaced by a heftier 799 cc vee-twin.

Specification

Make Raleigh. **Model** No 9. **Engine** 699 cc (77 × 75 mm bore and stroke) side-valve flat twin. **Tyres** 650 × 65 mm beaded-edge voiturette on flat-base rims, front and rear. **Frame** Brazed-lug duplex tubular cradle, with swinging-arm rear suspension, no damping. **Front forks** Brampton Biflex girders. **Brakes** Dummy vee-rim front, 6 in diameter drum rear. **Weight** 290 lb. **Wheelbase** 57½ in. **Manufacturer** Raleigh Cycle Co Ltd, Lenton Boulevard, Nottingham.

Above Beautifully engineered but expensive to produce, the rear-sprung flat-twin Raleigh had to give way to a cheaper vee-twin.
Right Front forks are Brampton Biflex, as used by many other makes of the period. The outside flywheel, tucked behind the primary chaincase, is unusual.
Far right The Amac carburettor bolts directly on to the timing chest, so the incoming mixture receives a preliminary warming.
Below For all its size, the Model 9 Raleigh is an undeniably pretty machine. Mainly, it was for the sidecar man.

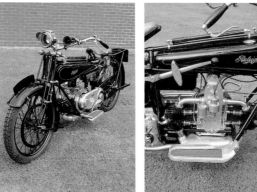

1939 1,140 cc Royal Enfield Model K

Except for the 1,150 cc Brough-Superior (of which only a few were made, anyway), the 1,140 cc Royal Enfield Model K was the most massive motorcycle available on the British pre-war market. But whereas the rider of to-day equates size with shattering speed, the big Enfield was not exceptional. Certainly it could be supplied to special order, with solo ratios in its four-speed gearbox, but sidecar gearing was standard, for the Model K's role in life was as a heavy haulier.

This was the machine to which a trader would attach a float to carry ladders, bags of cement, and the tools of a builder's business; it would carry a farmer's beasts to market; with a suitably decorated box chair, it sold ice-cream at the seaside on sunny summer Sundays; and, neglected and unkempt, with a plank tied to a bare sidecar chassis, it was a motorcycle dealer's hack, used to deliver or collect a customer's machine.

The Model K was the only bike in the 1939 Royal Enfield catalogue which still retained a hand gearchange. But who needed the slickness of a footchange on a bike like this, anyway? There had long been a 976 cc vee-twin in the Royal Enfield range, but in September 1936 the model underwent a complete redesign, to emerge as a sophisticated 1,140 cc model with dry-sump lubrication and the oil compartment cast integrally with the crankcase. Indeed, there were no fewer than *four* oil pumps, all with the oscillating plunger pattern which was a long-familiar Royal Enfield feature.

The oil pump fed the big-end bearings, another the front cylinder; the third pump delivered oil into the timing-gear housing, while the fourth returned surplus oil from the timing gear to the oil tank. Engine and gearbox were housed in a full duplex cradle frame, in which the front down tubes passed either side of the projecting crankcase oil container. An oil-bath primary chaincase was provided, but the clutch ran dry in a separate compartment. The catalogue price was £70, but for £5 extra the machine could have interchangeable wheels.

Normally, the Model K had a hand-operated clutch, but if required it could be supplied with American-style controls including a foot clutch. In October 1938, *Motor Cycling* road-tested the machine with a huge touring sidecar attached, and, with the chair occupied by a 14 stone passenger, the outfit clocked a respectable best-one-way speed of 62 mph, with a two-way mean of just over 58 mph. Fuel consumption was a bit disappointing, at 44 mpg on the open road.

Production of the Model K ended officially at the outbreak of war, the factory thereafter turning out thousands of 346 cc Model C and Model CO singles for military service. However, one more Model K was built, some time around 1941 — a rather special version, with a live rear axle and prop-shaft drive to the sidecar wheel of a military-style outfit similar to the Norton Big Four. It was an experiment, built in the hopes of attracting a military contract which, alas, failed to materialize. The Army, it seemed, had decided to abandon cross-country sidecars in favour of the Jeep.

Surprisingly, the sidecar-drive Model K was not scrapped, but with prop-shaft removed it served the factory for many years as a hack, carting spares until well into the 'fifties. It was then sold off, bought by private enthusiasts, and survives to this day rebuilt to its original military condition as a reminder of something that could well have worked, given a touch of encouragement from those in high places.

Specification

Make Royal Enfield. **Model** Model K. **Engine** 1,140 cc (85.5 × 99.25 mm bore and stroke) 50° side-valve vee-twin. **Tyres** 4.00 × 19 in, wired edge. **Frame** Brazed-lug duplex tubular loop. No rear springing. **Front forks** Centre-spring girders. **Brakes** Drums, 8 in diameter front and rear. **Weight** Not known. **Wheelbase** 59 in. **Manufacturer** Enfield Cycle Co Ltd, Hewell Road, Redditch, Worcs.

Above The size of the crankcase gives some indication of the huge diameter flywheels within, which endowed the Model K with tremendous torque.

Right Frame design is duplex-loop, the tubes passing each side of the vast oil-containing crankcase castings.

Far right Most Royal Enfield bikes employed Albion gearboxes, but the gearbox of the Model K appears to be of Burman make.

Below Nothing dainty or short-wheelbase about this one! The vast Model K was the largest machine ever built in quantity in Britain.

1961 692 cc Royal Enfield Constellation

An intriguing facet of Royal Enfield's parallel twin engine production is that all the units were manufactured deep in the bowels of the earth, in a wartime factory constructed from old limestone workings near Bradford-on-Avon, Wiltshire. Another part of the same workings served as a storehouse for priceless relics removed from London museums as a protection against bombs. True, the workers never saw daylight, but the advantage of the unusual factory was that the temperature remained virtually constant, winter or summer, allowing a precise standard of machining to be achieved.

Royal Enfield had entered the world of vertical twins late in 1948 with a 500 cc twin known quite simply as the 500 Twin, and it was from this model that all subsequent twin-cylinder Enfields were developed. The design differed from the usual Triumph-BSA-Ariel-Norton pattern in a number of ways. Oil, for instance, was carried in the sump; cylinder barrels and heads were individual, not cast *en bloc* and the barrels were very deeply sunk into the crankcase mouths. To allow the best possible air flow between the cylinders, the rockers were actuated by pushrods located at the four outer corners of the engine. That meant inlet and exhaust camshafts fore and aft, driven by a lengthy chain which also drove the rear-mounted dynamo.

Although the engine appeared to be in unit with the gearbox, this was not strictly so, for the Albion gearbox was bolted directly on to a flat face on the rear of the crankcase assembly. Royal Enfield were pioneers of post-war swinging-arm rear springing, and as proprietary hydraulic damper units were not yet in commercial production, they manufactured their own at first.

Royal Enfield included a 500 cc twin in the line-up right through to 1963, but in the meantime the demands for a greater-capacity model had become more and more strident. The first answer, in 1953, was the 692 cc Meteor, in effect, a doubling-up of the 346 cc Bullet single and using the same 70 × 90 mm dimensions. This led first to a redesigned version for 1956 bearing the Super Meteor name, then at last, two years later, to the Constellation, though the Super Meteor remained in the range as a slightly down-market model with a lower compression ratio, single carburettor, and a painted instead of chromium-plated front mudguard and fuel tank.

Internally, the Constellation employed a crankshaft which had been balanced both statically and dynamically. First examples had an 8.5 to 1 compression ratio, and twin Amal TT carburettors, but that was perhaps excessive, and for 1961 — the year of the machine featured here — there were Amal Monobloc carbs and an 8 to 1 ratio. Full-width wheel hubs, a Siamesed exhaust system, and low, flat handlebars gave the machine a sporty appearance which was reinforced by its performance.

It was capable of a top speed around 112 mph, and was raced in production events such as the Thruxton 500 miles, where Constellations finished second and third in the over-500 cc class in 1958. Outright success eluded them, however, even though the formidable Bob McIntyre tried hard for three years.

The Constellation was to remain in production until 1963, but in its final two years it was overtaken by a still bigger Enfield twin, the 736 cc Interceptor which was to survive even closure of the main Redditch factory, the final examples being built in that underground works at Bradford-on-Avon.

Specification

Make Royal Enfield. **Model** Constellation.
Engine 692 cc (70 × 90 mm bore and stroke) overhead-valve vertical twin.
Tyres 3.25 × 19 in front, 3.50 × 19 in rear.
Frame All-welded tubular diamond, with swinging-arm rear springing. **Front forks** Telescopic, hydraulically damped.
Brakes Drums, twin 6 in diameter at front, 7 in diameter at rear. **Weight** 403 lb.
Wheelbase 54 in. **Manufacturer** Enfield Cycle Co Ltd, Hewell Road, Redditch, Worcs.

Above Royal Enfield's standard-bearer, the powerful 692 cc Constellation never quite achieved the acclaim it should have. Unusually, the crankshaft was balanced both statistically and dynamically.

Right Front braking was by a full-width hub with a 6 in drum at each side, and it was most effective.

Far right Cylinder barrels (sunk deeply into the crankcase mouth) and light-alloy heads were individual, not cast *en bloc*.

Below Low, flat handlebars and an imposing tank give the 'Connie' a sporty aspect, which its performance does not belie.

1917 976 cc Royal Ruby 'Russian'

In the years immediately prior to the First World War, the Ruby Cycle Company was a relatively small business. Based in Ancoats, among the cotton mills of Manchester, and headed by George Rigby, the firm were primarily bicycle manufacturers, but from 1909 they had been building a 350 cc JAP-engined motorcycle and, gradually, the range.was extended until the top model was a handsome and powerful 976 cc side-valve vee-twin.

For 1915, there were two vee-twins, of 750 and 976 cc, and the company had begun to expand their activities, for both models were now equipped with a three-speed countershaft gearbox of Royal Ruby's own design and manufacture. Wartime contracts for munitions and components at first led to a toning-down of the motorcycle manufacturing side, but with the construction of a large new works at Moss Lane, Altrincham, on the south side of Manchester, there was again room to breathe and, gratefully, Royal Ruby began to accept contracts to supply the 976 cc twin to the Allies' governments (though not, apparently, to the War Office).

Moreover, in November of 1915 it was reported that the company had a 976 cc twin under development, equipped with a swinging-arm rear suspension system controlled by leaf springs. *The Motor Cycle's* man had a test ride in Manchester drizzle, over a particularly abominable stretch of greasy cobbles. 'There was no rattle,' he said, 'and even when ridden at high speed over the potholes no suggestion of jar was conveyed to the rider, though the road was so bad that the front forks bumped continuously.'

All the same, the conditions were not yet ripe for introducing the spring frame. (It was put into production after the war, but on Royal Ruby singles, not the twins.) The company was possibly unhappy with their own gearbox, for in 1916 it was supplanted by a Jardine, then in 1917 by a Sturmey-Archer.

Civilian sales of motorcycles in Britain had been banned at Easter 1916, and Royal Ruby's 1917 976 cc vee-twin was known as the 'Russian' model, because it was produced specifically to meet a request from the Russian Army's purchasing commission. Changes included a round-sided instead of flat-sided fuel tank, and the addition of a substantial tubular rear carrier which had an unusually long leather toolbag at each side.

Some of the twins were certainly despatched to Russia, but the outbreak of the Soviet Revolution meant that obtaining payment was difficult, and machines from the latter part of the order were diverted to other markets. A few, such as the one seen here, stayed in Britain.

Peacetime saw Royal Ruby roaring ahead, and now there was not only the promised spring frame but also, for the single-cylinder models, engines of their own manufacture. Hugh Gibson, later publicity manager of Raleigh, was appointed sales manager. But it seemed that the company was flying too high, for 1922 brought a resounding crash — the sell-up auction announcement including not only the premises and plant, but also the sales manager's car and the general manager's house!

The name and goodwill were bought by a Bolton company, and production restarted, but on a much smaller scale, and mainly with Villiers engines. The fade-out was gradual, the last year being 1933.

Specification

Make Royal Ruby. **Model** 8 hp. **Engine** JAP 976 cc (85.7 × 85 mm bore and stroke) 50° side-valve vee-twin. **Tyres** 650 × 65 mm beaded edge. **Frame** Brazed-lug tubular diamond, unsprung at rear. **Front forks** Brampton Biflex girders with horizontal and vertical movement. **Brakes** (non-standard) Drums, 7 in diameter, front and rear. **Weight** Not quoted. **Wheelbase** 62½ in. **Manufacturer** The Ruby Cycle Co Ltd, Moss Lane, Altrincham, Manchester.

Above The Royal Ruby was one of several makes of motorcycle to be built in Manchester, and for a while it was one of the best known. This is a First World War model, designed for the Russian Army.
Right Front forks are Brampton Biflex, sprung both vertically and horizontally.
Far right Engine is the inevitable 976 cc JAP, originating in Tottenham, North London; later, Royal Ruby built their own engines.
Below Drum brakes were not originally fitted to this model, and have been added by a previous owner.

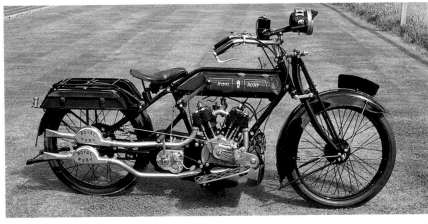

1913 750 cc Rudge Multi

It seems funny to give the name 'Multi' to a single-cylinder machine, but in this particular case we are not talking about a multiple number of cylinders, but the multiplicity of gear ratios that were available to the rider by courtesy of Rudge-Whitworth's patented belt-drive system. In fact, variations on the expanding-pulley system had been around almost from the very dawn of motorcycling, the idea being that if you pull the flanges of a vee-belt pulley apart, the belt sinks down and runs at a smaller diameter. The drawback to that, though, was that because the rear wheel pulley diameter stayed as it was, the belt ran slack and could slip.

It was John Pugh himself, the man who was to guide Rudge fortunes almost throughout the company's motorcycle manufacturing period, who came up with the idea of linking the driving and driven pulleys in such a way that as the flanges of one pulley were opened, those of the other one were closed accordingly, and belt tension remained constant. The actual range of ratios available was rather limited — from $3\frac{1}{2}$ to 1, to 7 to 1 — but it was an advantage over the earlier idea.

To operate the system, there was a huge lever on the left of the machine, operating in a tank-side quadrant which offered a choice of 24 notches. Of course, incorporation of a rear wheel pulley with a movable outer flange called for some ingenuity on the wheel-builder's part, for he had to lace in no fewer than 76 spokes.

After initial testing during the late part of 1911, the Rudge Multi went into production for the 1912 season, though a single-speed machine remained in the catalogue for those who mistrusted the newfangled device. At first, the Rudge Multi was a 499 cc model, but for 1913 a 750 cc version was added especially for the sidecar enthusiast, and it is one of these that is featured here. Surprisingly, perhaps, the 750 cc model retained the 85 mm bore of the 499 cc, but the stroke went up from 88 mm to a colossal 132 mm. The carburettor, which had been introduced into the Rudge range the previous year, was a Senspray — a matter of keeping it in the family, for the Senspray was a product of Charles H. Pugh, founder of the Atco lawn-mower business.

In the 1914 Senior TT, Cyril Pullin used a Multi to give Rudge their first Isle of Man victory, while four other riders of the make made it five finishers from six starters. Nevertheless, the countershaft gearbox was rapidly making headway, and the truth was that Rudge clung to the belt-drive Multi for too long. Indeed, when peace returned in 1919, they even added a 998 cc vee-twin, the Rudge Multwin. The Multi was still offered in the 1923 catalogue, but that was its final year, and for 1924 the four-valve, four-speed Rudge with all-chain drive was to take the factory into the modern world.

Nevertheless, a quotation from an early Rudge Multi handbook might raise an eyebrow or two. 'The best way to drive a Multi,' it says, 'is to get the engine turning round nicely on half throttle, and then drive entirely on the gear, moving the lever so that the engine does its work at almost constant speed.' So *that's* why there were 24 notches in the gear quadrant! But, continues the book, 'High gear .... affords most delightful quiet running on long descents and before the wind. This is like coasting. It lowers the petrol consumption and saves the wear and tear of the engine, and the carbon deposit is much reduced, as a relatively high road speed may be maintained while the engine fires slowly with a weak mixture.'

Specification

Make Rudge. **Model** Multi. **Engine** 750 cc (85 × 132 mm bore and stroke) inlet-over-exhaust single-cylinder. **Tyres** 26 × $2\frac{1}{4}$ in beaded-edge. **Frame** Brazed-lug diamond construction. No rear springing. **Front forks** Girder, with enclosed central spring. **Brakes** Bicycle-type stirrup front, belt-rim wedge rear. **Weight** 242 lb. **Wheelbase** 55 in. **Manufacturer** Rudge-Whitworth Ltd, Crow Lane, Coventry.

Above Essence of the Multi's gearing system is that as the flanges of the driving pulley close, so those of the rear wheel pulley open — and vice versa. A clever linkage ensures constant belt tension.

Right For all its sit-up-and-beg riding position, the big Multi was no 'slow-coach'.

Far right Valve layout is inlet-over-exhaust. Note the pedalling mechanism to start engine. The carburettor is a Senspray.

Below The silver tank distinguishes the pre-First World War Rudge Multi; post-war examples adopted a green tank finish.

1938 986 cc Scott Model 3S

On the face of it, a three-cylinder motorcycle engine might seem ideal, for with the cranks at 120° there would be evenly-spaced firing intervals and, thereby, a smooth-running motor. However, designers for the most part fought shy of the three because the layout also brought a vibration-producing end-to-end couple, in theory, anyway. Still, this did not really apply to a two-stroke engine using conventional crankcase primary compression, for in essence it comprised three single-cylinder units each with its own crank chamber.

William Cull, the Scott designer in the 1930s, was the first to bring out a three, at first as an experimental 747 cc machine, with the water-cooled engine in line with the frame. The crankcase was an Elektron magnesium box, into which was slid a crankshaft assembly comprising four light-alloy drums with main bearings serving to form the walls of the three crank chambers. A gearbox incorporating a car-type clutch was integral with the engine. The arrangement really cried out for shaft final drive, but Scott's settled instead for bevel gears to provide chain final drive.

That was in 1933, but the public waited in vain for news of impending production. The prototype, it seems, was less than perfect; indeed, test rider Allan Jefferies is reported to have said that on a straight road he had the greatest difficulty in keeping the machine from wandering from kerb to kerb! Back at the factory, a comprehensive redesign was undertaken, and the three which was finally unveiled at the 1934 Olympia Motor Cycle Show was a very different-looking animal.

Apart from an increase in capacity to 986 cc, the principle of the engine was unchanged, but it was now a much sleeker job with tidied-up castings, a four-speed foot-change gearbox and a complicated oiling system in which a throttle-controlled swashplate pump drew oil from the sump but delivered it through a gear-type pump, while another gear-type pump operated the scavenge side.

On the machine as exhibited at the show, the pannier fuel tanks were carried on the frame top tube, but this arrangement was changed later. Now there were tanks slung at each side of the rear mudguard, and louvered panelling (the sides of which hinged up, to give access to the upper half of the engine) faired into the radiator provided a dummy 'tank' which embodied an instrument panel.

The eventual price of the Model 3S was given as £115. The first 'production' model did not leave the Shipley works until 1936, and it is thought that not more than eight were built all told. The National Motorcycle Museum's example carries frame number 8 and engine number 3S.5008, so it was probably the last of all. As exhibited, it is equipped with a combination of swinging-arm and plunger rear springing, but this is not original, and was fitted at some time during the Second World War by Smokey Dawson of DMW.

Strangely enough, the last Model 3S was not the end of the Scott Three story. Many years later, in 1959, a further batch of three-cylinder engines was made, but in marine trim, for either inboard or outboard mounting. The prototypes were shown at the 1959 Boat Show, but again they failed to go into quantity production and so a possible spin-off in the form of a modern Scott Three remained no more than a pipe-dream.

Specification

Make Scott. **Model** 3S. **Engine** 986 cc (75 × 68.25 mm bore and stroke) water-cooled, in-line three-cylinder two-stroke. **Tyres** 3.25 × 20 in front and rear, wired edge. **Frame** All-welded channel-section steel, with DMW swinging-arm rear springing. **Front forks** Webb girders. **Brakes** Drums, 8 in diameter front and rear. **Weight** 490 lb. **Wheelbase** 60½ in. **Manufacturer** Scott Motor Cycle Co Ltd, Saltaire, Shipley, Yorkshire.

Above Plunger rear springing is not original, but was added by DMW during the Second World War.

Right Eye-catching indeed are the radiators, which merge into the front part of the dummy tank.

Far right Despite the massive build of the engine, the castings are very tidy. Designer was William Cull.

Below Only eight examples of the water-cooled Scott straight-three two-stoke were ever built, and this was probably the last one of all. The 'fuel tank' above the engine is a dummy, fuel being contained instead in pannier tanks each side of the rear wheel.

1935 649 cc Triumph Model 6/1 Twin

If you were asked which British factory was first in the field with a production vertical twin, you would probably answer Triumph, with Edward Turner's immortal 500 cc Speed Twin of 1938. But this would only be half right. Certainly the firm was Triumph, but several years before the arrival of Edward Turner, the man in the design office was Val Page, and it was he who brought out a very sturdy six-fifty, the Model 6/1.

It must be said, however, that the old Triumph company did not seem to push the 650 cc twin very hard in contemporary advertising. It was considered principally as a sidecar haulier, and indeed, there was a very cunning arrangement of a plunger and ratchet at the rear of the primary chaincase, by means of which the rear brake could be locked on to prevent a parked combination from rolling back when on a slope.

Moreover, it was a very heavy-looking machine with a deep tank and many extra heavy-duty features and although foot-change gearboxes were very popular in the mid-'thirties, the big twin stuck to a massive tank-side hand-change lever. Only in its final year was footchange offered as an optional extra, in a rather half-hearted manner.

However, it was still considered to be an outstanding design. Page was breaking new ground, and all the model really needed was the touch of a cosmetician. Sales manager Harry Perrey did his best. A showman as well as a trials man of repute, he even drove a specially-prepared 6/1 outfit through the International Six Days Trial of 1933, soon after the machine was launched, but before 'The Motor Cycle' was given a chance to try it out. It was not a full-scale road test, but it was enough to impress the reporter concerned, who commented favourably on the coupled front and rear brakes, the silent-running double helical gears of the primary drive — which meant, incidentally, that the engine actually ran 'wrong way round' — and the neat way in which semi unit-construction was obtained by bolting the gearbox directly to a facing on the rear of the crankcase assembly.

One way in which the Val Page twin dif-
fered from the later Edward Turner model was that it had just a single camshaft at the rear of the cylinder block, very similar to the Norton Dominator. The pistons rose and fell together, and the one-piece crankshaft had three integral bobweights. Split plain big-end bearings were white-metal lined. The lubrication system was dry-sump, with the oil carried in the base of the crankcase, a large filler neck being provided at the right-hand front.

A satisfactory machine all round, but Turner had his own twin on the stocks, and that is why the 6/1 had to be dropped.

Specification

Make Triumph. **Model** 6/1. **Engine** 649 cc (70 × 84 mm bore and stroke) overhead-valve parallel twin. **Tyres** 3.50 × 19 in front and rear. **Frame** Brazed-lug duplex cradle. No rear springing. **Front forks** Tubular girders. **Brakes** Drums, coupled, 8 in diameter front and rear. **Weight** Not quoted. **Wheelbase** 54 in. **Manufacturer** Triumph Company Ltd, Priory Street, Coventry.

Above Primary drive was by gears, which meant the engine ran 'backwards'. A pawl and ratchet at the rear of the primary-drive casing locked on the brakes for parking.
Right It was poor styling that killed the Page twin, which had a very heavy look, however worthy it may have been.
Far right Unlike the Turner twin, the Val Page version had a single camshaft at the rear of the block, and carried oil in the sump.
Below Triumph were certainly first in the field with a vertical twin — but it was a Val Page model, a few years before Edward Turner's better-known Speed Twin.

1950 649 cc Triumph 6T Thunderbird

It was in September 1949 that a dramatic new Triumph was announced, bearing a name straight from the mythology of the North American Indian. This was the 649 cc Thunderbird — and incidentally, when Ford later introduced a car with the same model name, they had the courtesy to ask Triumph for permission.

Background to the introduction was the persistent clamour from Triumph dealers in the USA for a more powerful model than the existing 500 cc twins, with stamina enough for America's vast highways. Edward Turner's answer was to build an enlarged version of his Speed Twin, using Speed Twin parts so far as was practicable. However, both bore and stroke dimensions were increased, the Thunderbird producing in its original form a useful 34 bhp at 6,300 rpm.

Unfortunately for Triumph, the coming of the new model coincided with a world nickel shortage, so instead of a flamboyant chromium-plated tank the bike was given an unusual all-over finish in steel grey-blue, enlivened by a chromium-plated horizontal styling band at each side of the tank.

By this time the Triumph people had acquired a considerable flair for publicity, and the Thunderbird was given a spectacular launch when three of the new models were ridden from the works to the Montlhéry Autodrome near Paris (France's equivalent of Brooklands). There, under official ACU observation, all three machines were set to average 90 mph for 500 miles, which they achieved magnificently, the trio completing a final lap at over 100 mph. This, by the way, was on the only fuel currently obtainable — a low-quality 72 octane that would not even rate as One Star on today's scale, and which meant running on a compression ratio no higher than 7 to 1.

At this time, the standard Triumph frame still had a rigid rear end, but Turner craftily introduced a sprung hub, that is a wheel with an oversize hub within which shock and rebound springs were housed. Wheel movement was pretty minimal, but the beauty of the sprung hub, from Triumph's viewpoint, was that it gave the customer some kind of springing, without the factory having to throw out all the old frame jigs and manufacture new ones. Incredibly, Triumph were to go direct from sprung hub to swinging-arm suspension, the only plunger-sprung models being the small Terrier and Tiger Club singles.

For 1950, the year of the machine in our pictures, a Mk II sprung hub was put into production, with conventional ball journal bearings and integral oil seals. In other respects, however, the machine was as before. In the years ahead there would be some interesting changes including, for 1952, use of an SU carburettor which afforded quite remarkable economy. Indeed, in a special effort five laps of a ten-mile road circuit were covered at 155 mpg, at an average speed of 30 mph. Under normal give-and-take conditions, something more like 90 mpg was attained.

Specification

Make Triumph. **Model** 6T Thunderbird. **Engine** 649 cc (71 × 82 mm bore and stroke) overhead-valve parallel twin. **Tyres** 3.25 × 19 in front, 3.50 × 19 in rear, wired-edge. **Frame** All-welded tubular cradle, with internally-sprung rear wheel hub. **Front forks** Telescopic, hydraulically damped. **Brakes** Drums, 7 in diameter front, 8 in diameter rear. **Weight** 397 lb. **Wheelbase** 55 in. **Manufacturer** Triumph Engineering Co Ltd, Meriden Works, Allesley, Coventry.

Above Introduction of the Thunderbird coincided with a world nickel shortage, which meant that the tank had to be painted instead of plated — but the steel grey finish was very distinctive.

Right Adding to the glamour of the Thunderbird was the streamlined headlamp nacelle incorporated in the front forks.

Far right The first 649 cc Triumph engine was a derivative of the 498 cc Speed Twin, but as the years passed so development continued along its own path.

Below The Thunderbird is fitted with Edward Turner's patented sprung rear hub — heavy, and with only limited movement.

1960 649 cc Triumph T120 Bonneville

Few indeed are the motorcycles of this world which have been so loved by their riders as to be given a nickname — but the 'Bonnie' is one such, and the name became so well-known that it was adopted as the title of a book by John Nelson, former Triumph service manager, describing the Bonneville's development history.

It all started with the Thunderbird, first of the post-Second World War 649 cc Triumph twins. From that the more sporty Tiger 110 evolved, with higher compression ratio, bigger valves and ports, and a sports camshaft. But in time the demand grew for a machine with still more performance, and so the experimental department at Meriden works began work on a new twin-carburettor version of the 649 cc twin, to be introduced for the 1959 season.

To date it had no particular name, but Triumph had certainly not forgotten the tremendous achievement of Johnny Allen who, on Bonneville Salt Flats in the USA, had taken a cigar-shaped projectile, powered by an unsupercharged Triumph Thunderbird engine (running on a hair-raising brew of nitro-methane) to a record-breaking 214.4 mph. As a tribute to Allen's sterling effort, the new sports twin would be called the T120 Bonneville.

The first Bonnie became a last-minute addition to the Triumph range as displayed at the 1958 Earl's Court Show. It featured the traditional 'nacelle' headlamp enclosure at the top of the front forks, but it was eye-catching none the less, with an unexpected tank finish of tangerine and grey. At this stage the frame was the usual Thunderbird-type, with a single front down tube, but during the first year of production a number of minor modifications were made.

Not until the 1960 season (and it is a 1960 model we see here) did the Bonnie begin to take on the form by which it would be recognized by countless enthusiasts. Particularly noticeable was the new duplex cradle frame, the separate headlamp and the lighter-looking telescopic front forks, with distinguishing rubber bellows to keep out the dust. A tachometer was not yet fitted as a standard item, but a tachometer drive kit was soon made available, the drive being taken from the timing-chest end of the exhaust camshaft.

Understandably, contestants in production-machine racing saw the advent of the Bonneville as the fulfilment of their dreams. 'The Bonnie owner,' said *The Motor Cycle*, 'is he who has taken a deep breath and inhaled oodles of enthusiasm.' The Thruxton 500-Miler, the Hutchinson 100, the Isle of Man Production TT: all became feathers in the Bonnie's cap. John Hartle made history by winning the first Production Machine TT; Malcolm Uphill added another chapter by winning the 1967 event at 99.99 mph after twice making 100 mph laps.

As the years passed, so the Bonneville remained at the top of the Triumph twin production list. By 1962 it had adopted unit construction instead of the original separate engine and gearbox. Frame design was revised yet again, to give more rigidity to the rear swinging-arm pivot. Electrics became first conventional 12 volts then in time electronic ignition was added.

Surviving the collapse of the original company and the setting up of a workers' co-operative, the Bonneville was still being manufactured in the late 1980s, not at Meriden where the site of the now-demolished factory had become a housing estate, but at Newton Abbott in Devon.

Specification

Make Triumph. **Model** T120 Bonneville.
Engine 649 cc (71 × 82 mm bore and stroke) overhead-valve parallel twin.
Tyres 3.25 × 19 in front, 3.50 × 19 in rear, wired edge. **Frame** All-welded duplex cradle with swinging-arm rear springing, hydraulically damped. **Front forks** Telescopic, hydraulically damped. **Brakes** Drums, 8 in diameter front, 7 in diameter rear. **Weight** 395 lb. **Wheelbase** 55¾ in. **Manufacturer** Triumph Engineering Co Ltd, Meriden Works, Allesley, Coventry.

Above The bike that looked as though it was doing 70 when standing still! This is the potent Triumph Bonneville as it wil be remembered by many a dad and granddad of today.

Right A two-tone finish was available from the start, the colours changing over the years.

Far right Seen in this view are the die-cast light-alloy cylinder head, and the tachometer drive (an extra-cost item) driven from the end of the exhaust camshaft.

Below First of the Bonnevilles to take on recognizable 'Bonnie' features — separate chromed headlamp, new duplex cradle frame, and bellows to the telescopic front forks.

1975 744 cc Triumph T160 Trident

In one respect, the T160 Triumph Trident was the end of a legend. It was the last machine to be designed under the banner of the old BSA Group, and the last model to be built at the famous Small Heath plant before that disappeared under the demolition–men's sledgehammers. But it was a *Triumph*, so why mention BSA and Small Heath?

In 1969, there were two three-cylinder motorcycles: one had the engine mounted with the cylinder block sitting vertically, and the name Triumph on the tank; the other had the cylinder block mounted forward, and the tank said BSA. But really they were the same basic design, and the engines for both were built at the BSA works.

Design was a joint effort involving Bert Hopwood and Doug Hele, and a three-cylinder engine was chosen because with the crankpins set at 120° the even firing intervals would give an exceptionally smooth-running motor. True, this could have had the disadvantage of an end-to-end couple, but this danger turned out to be more apparent than real. What was particularly ingenious was the way in which the three-throw crankshaft was produced. It was a forging, and initially the three crank throws were all in a line; but then the shaft was held fast in the centre, one end was twisted one way, the other end the other way. In other respects the Triumph Trident and the equivalent BSA Rocket 3 could be considered as a 'Tiger 100 and a half' for the layout was entirely Triumph, with camshafts located fore and aft of the cylinders.

The cylinder block was a light-alloy casting with pressed-in iron liners, and the forged light-alloy connecting rods, with car-type big-end bearing shells, were an echo of those of the Bonneville. An outstanding feature of the early threes was the 'ray gun' silencer, with three miniature tail pipes at each side.

The Meriden dispute and the blockade by striking workers certainly hit the Triumph Trident, because although the engine was a Small Heath product, the frame was built and assembly carried out at Meriden. But with the company falling into the hands of the new Norton-Villiers-Triumph combine, duplicate sets of frame jigs had to be manufactured and installed at Small Heath. The BSA name was dropped, and when the posters went up on the railings of the former BSA plant, the message they gave was that 'Triumphs are rolling again!'

The NVT group established a new experimental department at Kitts Green, Birmingham, and it was there, under the guidance of Doug Hele, that the final Triumph Trident design emerged for the 1975 season. This was the Model T160 which, with the Rocket 3 now deceased, employed the former sloping-forward BSA version of the three; a nicely-rounded fuel tank replaced the old slab-sided tank, and new cylindrical silencers superseded the 'ray guns'. More importantly, an electric starter had been incorporated for the first time which engaged with a pinion at the rear of the clutch drum.

Production came to a halt at the end of 1975, the example shown here being one of the last made, but as the last machine came down the Small Heath line, the workers gave it a fitting farewell — by affixing BSA transfers to it!

Specification

Make Triumph. **Model** T160 Trident. **Engine** 744 cc (67 × 70 mm bore and stroke). **Tyres** 4.10 × 19 in, front and rear, wired edge. **Frame** All-welded duplex cradle, with swinging-arm rear suspension, hydraulically damped. **Front forks** Telescopic, hydraulically damped. **Brakes** Single discs, front and rear. **Weight** 503 lb. **Wheelbase** 58 in. **Manufacturer** Norton Villiers Triumph Ltd, Armoury Road, Small Heath, Birmingham 10.

Above Very effective annular-ring silencers were developed by the Norton-Villiers-Triumph group. Within the primary chaincase is a diaphragm-type clutch.

Right Matched speedometer and tachometer 'binnacles' are attractive.

Far right The forwardly-inclined engine was originally a BSA Rocket Three feature, but was adopted by Triumph after BSA production ceased.

Below Last of the Triumph-BSA three-cylinder models, the T160 Trident had achieved an air of supreme elegance. Note the electric starter motor located above the gearbox.

1937 998 cc Vincent-HRD Series A Rapide

There is a legend among Vincent folk that the vee-twin Rapide was the outcome of a happy accident. One day in 1936, it is said, designer Phil Irving happened to place a tracing of the company's 500 cc single on top of a drawing of the same engine's timing-side, in such a way that a vision of a narrow angle vee-twin came to light.

Legend or not, there was a practical reason for choosing a 47° angle between the cylinders, for it meant that by reversing the drilling jig for the cylinder mounting studs, the stud holes for the second cylinder could be produced without further expenditure. The idler gear of the single was offset from the cylinder centre-line by $23\frac{1}{2}$°, so it was convenient to give the twin a 47° angle.

In pre-war days the name on the tank was Vincent-HRD rather than plain Vincent because to make his entry into the market Phil Vincent had bought-up the defunct HRD trade mark from the successors to TT-winner Howard R. Davies's company. However, only the name was the same, and there was no other connection between the original HRD models and Phil's rear-sprung Vincent-HRDs.

The Series A Rapide was a surprise announcement for the 1937 season. 'The idea behind the design,' said the contemporary press, 'is the production of an exceptionally lively, high-performance mount with the same superb handling as the smaller models in the range. Not only this, but the makers have aimed at providing a 100 mph machine that is docile and does not rely on super-tuning for its out-of-the-ordinary capabilities or require an ultra-high compression ratio.'

The new Rapide adopted the cantilever rear springing system already made famous on the single-cylinder Vincent HRDs, and which, indeed, would still be featured on the very last Vincents of all, some years later. Unusually advanced for 1937, the machine had a stainless-steel tank, twin brakes on both wheels, and a duplex primary chain. The gearbox was a four-speed Burman.

Enthusiasts soon named the Rapide the 'plumber's nightmare' because of the tangle of externally-mounted copper oil pipes, but at least it was fairly oil-tight by the standards of the day, and in practice it did live up to its promise of effortless high performance. As an example, George Brown, a name long to be associated with deeds of derring-do on Vincent twins, rode one in *The Motor Cycle*'s 1937 Brooklands Clubman's Day, and was clocked at almost 113 mph.

Motorcycle production was halted during the First World War, so the Vincent-HRD company worked on a number of interesting projects aimed at aiding the war effort, but teaser advertisements in the motorcycling press hinted that a redesigned Rapide would be available when peace returned.

This turned out to be the Series B Rapide, which retained a number of features of the pre-war model, such as dual brakes, cantilever rear springing and 84 × 90 mm bore and stroke, but in a much refined package. No longer did the 'plumber's nightmare' jibe apply, for the engine — now with 50° cylinder angle — was provided with internal oilways. The Series B was followed by the Series C, and eventually by the Series D, but that's another story...

Specification

Make Vincent-HRD. **Model** Series A Rapide. **Engine** 998 cc (84 × 90 mm bore and stroke) 47° overhead-valve vee-twin. **Tyres** 3 × 20 in front, 3 × 19 in rear. **Frame** Brazed-lug duplex tubular cradle. Cantilever rear springing. **Front forks** Centre-spring girders. **Brakes** Twin drums, 7 in diameter front and rear. **Weight** 400 lb. **Wheelbase** $58\frac{1}{2}$ in. **Manufacturer** The Vincent-HRD Co Ltd, Great North Road, Stevenage, Herts.

Above As in all Phil Vincent's machines from start to finish, the rear fork assembly is sprung cantilever-fashion, with springs under the seat.

Right Front forks are conventional centre-spring girders, but twin front drum brakes are unexpected.

Far right Angle between the cylinders of the pre-war Rapide is only 47° hence the cramped appearance. Note the exposed hairpin valve springs.

Below First of the Vincent vee-twins, the Series A Rapide was termed the 'plumber's nightmare' — and not undeservedly, from the look of all that external oil piping!

1955 998 cc Vincent Series D Black Shadow

Strictly speaking, Vincent had not intended to build a Series D version of the Black Shadow, and that they did indeed do so was due to force of circumstances. But let's start with the 4 November 1954 issue of *The Motor Cycle*, since any enthusiast flipping through the pages of that issue would have sat up with a start on reaching page 578.

'Startling Vincent Developments', ran the headline, and that was certainly true. Phil Vincent was determined that the new season's models would be the ultimate in gentlemanly riding, so here was a range clad from head to tail in shiny black glass-fibre panelling; not that everybody approved, and there was a sizeable body who claimed that to encase that gloriously macho vee-twin engine smacked of sacrilege.

Still, underneath the bodywork the mechanics were much as before, and the top-of-the-range 998 cc twin, now named the Black Prince, was really the familiar Black Shadow in heavy disguise. However, the 'frame', if such it was, had been redesigned, and no longer did the oil tank do extra duty as part of the structure, but it had been moved to a position under the seat, and replaced by a tubular member that in turn permitted use of a larger, four-gallon fuel tank.

The front forks were still Vincent Girdraulics, but instead of the customary, slim, Vincent-made damper units at the rear of the fork legs there were now heftier Armstrong units. Similarly, although the famous cantilever rear springing was retained, a single Armstrong damper (which, incidentally, allowed a full 6 in rear wheel movement) replaced Vincent's twin-unit arrangement.

Rear and prop stands now gave way to a centre stand operated by a hand lever, as on Rudges of the 1930s. Ribbed brake drums were fitted, two at the front, one at the rear. Engine modifications were few, the major being the adoption for the first time of coil ignition, claimed to be particularly beneficial to the twins in terms of easy starting and slow running; and for convenience of manufacture the same cylinder head was fitted to both front and rear cylinders.

But they say there is many a slip between cup and lip, and although the enclosed Vincents created a terrific sensation when shown at Earl's Court, the company ran into difficulty on the production line. The glass-fibre work was produced under contract by an outside firm, and the first examples delivered to Vincents were far from perfect. A new contract was negotiated with a company building car bodies in glass-fibre. This time the results were satisfactory, but in the meantime the Vincent assembly line had come to a stop. To keep the factory working, therefore, Phil Vincent brought out something that had not been envisaged — a stopgap range of naked Series D models, which reverted to their pre-plastic names of Comet, Rapide, and Black Shadow. It is, then, an undressed Series D Black Shadow that we see here, and immediately noticeable is the bench-type dual seat, and the somewhat angular tubular framework that had to be added to carry it.

Sadly, the Series D ended the Vincent line. Only 460 machines were built during 1955, the last of all being wheeled off the assembly line on 16 December 1955. For a few more years they carried on in other fields, but a disastrous venture into water-scooter manufacture heralded the end.

Specification

Make Vincent. **Model** Series D Black Shadow. **Engine** 998 cc (84 × 90 mm bore and stroke) 50° overhead-valve vee-twin. **Tyres** 3.50 × 19 in front, 4.00 × 18 in rear, wired edge. **Frame** None in accepted sense, engine unit forming bulk of frame and secured to tubular upper member at cylinder heads. Cantilever rear suspension, hydraulically damped. **Front forks** Vincent Girdraulic girders, assisted by hydraulic damper units. **Brakes** Drums, two 7 in diameter front, one 7 in diameter rear. **Weight** 447 lb. **Wheelbase** 56½ in. **Manufacturer** Vincent Engineers Ltd, Great North Road, Stevenage, Herts.

Above Immediately noticeable is the bench-type dual seat, necessitated by frame changes.
Right Front forks are still the familiar Girdraulics, but with Armstrong instead of Vincent's own damper struts.
Far right In this view the traditional Black Shadow engine is seen, but in fact the frame design had changed drastically.
Below Phil Vincent hadn't intended to build 'naked' bikes in 1955 and had planned a range totally enclosed in glass-fibre; but the shell manufacturer let him down, and the Series D as seen here was introduced to keep the factory occupied.

1950 998 cc Watsonian-JAP (Prototype)

You could well say that the most surprising machine in the entire National Motorcycle Museum collection is the lovely pale-green vee-twin which, attached to a luxurious open single-seater sidecar, stands in the foyer of the museum building. The sidecar is a Watsonian; but surprisingly so is the motorcycle! In fact, it is the only motorcycle ever made by the famous Watsonian company, founded over 75 years ago by joiner Fred Watson, and there was sound reasoning behind its construction.

In pre-war days, most motorcycle makers listed a hefty side-valve vee-twin especially for the family man, but when peace returned in the late 1940s the breed appeared to have died out. As Ron Watson, son of the founder, expressed it, 'If only Brough-Superior had returned to the market, there would have been no need to consider motor-cycle manufacture ourselves. But...we felt there was still a place for a big side-valve twin, though it would certainly be a limited field, and so we got in touch with the JAP company. The year was 1948, and it so happened that they already had a prototype engine that sounded exactly the kind we were looking for.'

The prototype JAP was a 50° twin producing around 35 bhp, and it incorporated an alternator instead of direct-current dynamo, plus coil-ignition and a car-type distributor. Design was a team effort, comprising Ron Watson, Tim Reid and to some extent Eric Oliver. Watsonian's spent a considerable amount of money in developing the machine, and when they felt they had it almost right, they asked JAP to quote for a supply of engines. But there lay the snag...

Seemingly, Watsonian's were the only potential customers for that particular power plant, and unless they could place a firm order for 500, the JAP works did not think it worth their while to tool up for production. That meant Watsonian's committing themselves to an outlay of £50,000 for engines alone, and they had not that much spare capital. By that time it was 1950, orders for sidecars were flooding in, and so the idea was shelved temporarily, though it

turned out to be permanently.

The Watsonian twin scored a motorcycle first in being equipped with a twin-leading-shoe front brake, with a hydraulic brake in a full-width drum at the rear. The fuel tank holds a massive $5\frac{1}{4}$ gallons, but even more impressive is the ribbed, cast-light-alloy oil tank to the rear of the gearbox, holding $1\frac{1}{4}$ gallons of lubricant. The telescopic front fork ends are also light-alloy castings, and although the fork looks conventional enough in fact it is a Dunlop experimental component with rubber-in-compression as the suspension medium.

Almost as interesting is the sidecar, for it is a Watsonian Monaco with no chassis as such. Instead, the centre section is of metal construction, reinforced to carry the attachment struts and the sidecar wheel, while the nose and tail components are in glass-fibre. Development of the Monaco chair, the first sidecar in the world to employ glass-fibre in its construction, was contemporary with the Watsonian motorcycle and therefore is a very appropriate companion.

Finally, do you recognize the pale-green paintwork? It is 'mist green', BSA Bantam green or, if you prefer, Sunbeam S7 Green — and it was chosen simply because Watsonian's had a drum of it especially to paint sidecars that were to be attached to Sunbeam S7s.

Specification

Make Watsonian. **Model** Prototype. **Engine** JAP 998 cc (80 × 99 mm bore and stroke) 50° side-valve vee-twin. **Tyres** 3.50 × 19 in front and rear. **Frame** Bronze-welded duplex tubular loop, with plunger rear springing. **Front forks** Dunlop telescopic, rubber-in-compression. **Brakes** 9 in diameter drums, front and rear; hydraulic operation of rear brake. **Weight** Not known. **Wheelbase** 58 in. **Manufacturer** Watsonian Sidecars Ltd, Albion Road, Greet, Birmingham.

Above Perhaps the most unexpected motorcycle in the whole museum, the vast Watsonian twin was built by the celebrated sidecar manufacturers. Sidecar is a Watsonian Monaco with glass-fibre allied to a metal centre section.

Right The front fork is not the usual hydraulically-damped affair, but is an experimental Dunlop incorporating rubber in shear.

Far right The light-alloy 998 cc JAP engine employed coil ignition. Unhappily, Watsonians could not order sufficient to make tooling-up for production worth while.

Below Note the ribbed cast-light-alloy oil tank to the rear of the gearbox.

1912 848 cc Wilkinson-TMC

Magnificent is the only word to describe the four-in-line Wilkinson, product of the same firm who today manufacture razor blades and garden implements. Just consider the specification; a four-cylinder water-cooled engine, shaft final drive, full rear springing by means of four laminated leaf springs, and the most comfortable-looking bucket seat of all time. Yet the biggest surprise of all must be the date of manufacture, for the example seen here was built as long ago as 1912. Indeed, the first Wilkinson four was exhibited at the 1909 Stanley Show, and manufacture continued (at a slow rate, admittedly; only around 250 Wilkinsons were built in all) until wartime restrictions on civilian production brought the venture to a close in the spring of 1916.

Wilkinson's were sword manufacturers by tradition — they still are, indeed — and to launch out into motorcycle production may seem a little odd, but the reason was that the bike was conceived as a military scouting machine. The designer was P.G. Tacchi, who was granted patent rights on a machine with shaft drive and full springing in 1908. At that time, the power unit was a transverse vee-twin, and in that guise the Wilkinson was demonstrated to the Army authorities in the summer of 1908 with a Maxim machine gun on the handlebars. It seems the Army was not impressed, but Wilkinson did not give up hope.

A new version was exhibited at the 1909 Stanley Show, this time with an air-cooled 676 cc four-cylinder engine, primarily as a luxurious tourer (it was termed the TAC, meaning Touring Auto Cycle). In addition, though, a military model was displayed, equipped with a water bottle, map case, binoculars, rifle clips and a revolver holster at the side of the seat. The air-cooled TAC was produced for the next couple of years, but in December 1911 the power unit was redesigned to accommodate water cooling, with a radiator carried across the front of the machine. The early model had used automatic inlet valves, but the water-cooled version had a conventional side-valve with a capacity of 848 cc. To mark the change, the TAC label was dropped in favour of TMC (for Touring Motor Cycle).

By mid-1913, the Wilkinson Sword Company became interested in a light car known as the Deemster which employed a 996 cc four-cylinder engine, and a bonus resulting from this development was that for sidecar use, a 996 cc version of the motorcycle now became available. There was, also, a Wilkinson-designed sidecar of majestic proportions, carried on parallel leaf springs similar to those used at the rear of the bike.

The machine seen here is one of the redesigned models announced for 1912, featuring a rear hub driven by bevel gearing instead of the original worm and worm-wheel, and Saxon forks instead of the earlier Druid or Wilkinson types. It is non-standard in one respect, namely the oil tank is mounted under the left footboard, from which a heel-operated pump supplies the lubricant to a glass sight-feed mounted above the frame top tube. The triangular tank between the frame tubes carries water only, while fuel is supplied from the crescent-shaped tank over the rear mudguard.

The outbreak of the First World War naturally saw Wilkinson hard at work in their traditional role of makers of swords and bayonets for the Army. With peace, the four-cylinder engine came back as the power unit of the Deemster car; but the bike never did.

Specification

Make Wilkinson. **Model** TMC. **Engine** 848 cc (60 × 75 mm bore and stroke) water-cooled four-cylinder side-valve. **Tyres** 26 × 2½ in beaded edge, front and rear. **Frame** Brazed-lug tubular construction, with quarter-elliptic leaf rear springing. **Front forks** Saxon girders, with horizontal spring compressed through bell-crank levers. **Brakes** No front brake. Twin rear drum brakes, operated by two pedals on right. **Weight** 320 lb. **Wheelbase** 62 in. **Manufacturer** The Wilkinson Sword Co Ltd, Southfield Road, Acton, London.

Above Made by the world-renowned sword and razor blade company, the 1912 Wilkinson-TMC straight four had an extremely sophisticated specification, including full springing, shaft drive, and a luxurious seat!

Right The front forks on this model are of Saxon manufacture, but Wilkinson also fitted Druids, and forks of their own design.

Far right The 'TMC' initials, as cast on the crankcase, stood for 'Touring Motor Cycle'. This is the water-cooled version, a straightforward side-valve.

Below Fuel is carried in the tank above the rear mudguard. The tank above the engine carries water.

1913 964 cc Williamson Flat Twin

Although the Coventry-built Williamson did not remain in production for very long, it was certainly one of the more intriguing machines of the immediate pre-First World War era. Its instigator was Billy Williamson, a colourful character who had been managing director of the Rex company (where his brother Harold was sales manager), but a board-room shake-up in October 1911 led to the resignation of both brothers.

Harold was immediately taken on by the Singer company, but within a few months there were rumours flying around that Billy was about to become a manufacturer in his own right. The capital for such a venture, it seems, was provided by none other than William Douglas, and when the first pro-totypes of the new machine appeared in April 1912, they were named Williamson-Douglas — with William Douglas junior and Harold Williamson as the test riders.

At this point, Douglas themselves were building 348 cc flat twins, but they were also about to go into production with a 964 cc Douglas cyclecar. The water-cooled 964 cc engine was equally suitable for powering a big sidecar-hauling bike, which is where Billy Williamson came into the picture; building the engine at Bristol for both the light car and the bike would help spread development and production costs.

The cyclecar origin of the power unit was very evident when the first production Williamson twins hit the market, for there was a dog on the timing-side end of the crankshaft, to which a detachable crank han-dle was applied for starting purposes. The gearbox was an oversize Douglas two-speeder, equipped with a foot-operated clutch, and the gears were changed by the usual Douglas 'tram handle' mounted across the top of the tank. The front fork was a Douglas-Druid, using two side-mounted springs in tension. Brakes were the William-son's weak point, for the front brake was simply a bicycle-type stirrup with blocks operating on the wheel rim, while at the rear was a contracting band brake worked by a heel pedal.

For 1913, the year of the example seen here, there were a few minor improvements such as a cush-drive rear sprocket, and a revised positioning of the carburettor (which now faced inward and was protected from accidental damage by the fuel tank). The price of the water-cooled twin was £82, but there was now a cheaper model with air-cooled cylinders — and, of course, without the honeycomb radiator — at £75.

A year later, further improvements em-braced a new timing cover which eliminated the starting handle dog (unnecessary now, because a kick-starter had been added) and the option of a three-speed gearbox. But the coming of war in August 1914 brought the end of the Williamson flat twin. When peace returned in 1919, the flat-twin Douglas engine was no longer available, and Billy Williamson redesigned the machine to take a 980 cc side-valve air-cooled JAP engine. The post-war Williamson was announced for 1920, but it is believed that no more than a dozen were made before tragedy struck. Billy suffered a fatal heart attack, and the business closed almost as soon as it had re-opened. For a while the former service manager con-tinued to operate a spares service from the Williamson works in Moor Street, Coventry, but then that, too, finished.

It was a sad end for a make which had car-ried with pride on its royal blue tank side panels the elephant-and-lynx coat of arms of the City of Coventry.

Specification

Make Williamson. **Model** Flat twin.
Engine 964 cc (85 × 85 mm bore and stroke) water-cooled Douglas horizontal side-valve twin. **Tyres** 26 × 3 in beaded-edge, front and rear. **Frame** Brazed-lug duplex tubular cradle. No rear springing. **Front forks** Douglas-Druid girders, with side-mounted coil springs in tension. **Brakes** Stirrup at front, contracting band at rear. **Weight** 300 lb. **Wheelbase** 60½ in. **Manufacturer** The Williamson Motor Company, Moor Street, Earlsdon, Coventry.

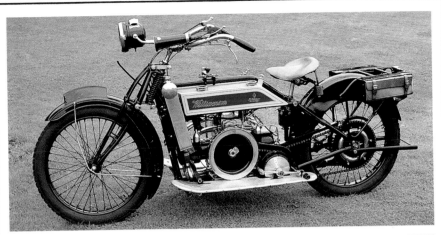

Above The Williamson company did survive the Great War, but Billy Williamson died just as the first post-war models were being made.

Right The Douglas factory co-operated keenly in the design of the Williamson, as they were themselves developing the engine for a light car.

Far right Starting was by means of a crank handle which engaged with a dog protruding from the timing chest, and not until the following year did the Williamson gain a kick-starter.

Below Built in Coventry by Billy Williamson, the 964 cc Williamson twin employed a water-cooled Douglas engine and Douglas gearbox.

1928 680 cc Zenith 'Six-Eighty'

Look closely at the Zenith trade mark as shown on the rear mudguard transfer, and you will see that it is a representation of a motorcycle imprisoned behind the bars of a gaol, with the word 'Barred' written across it. The reference is actually to the earlier Zenith-Gradua gearing system which, in the days when most bikes were single-geared, was considered to give Gradua owners so much of an advantage in hill-climbs and similar competitions that Zenith machines were banned from taking part.

Far from taking offence, the Zenith company were so delighted that they used the 'Barred' slogan in a highly-successful publicity campaign! However, the belt-drive Zenith Gradua was already history by the time the handsome purple-and-black twin featured here was manufactured. The makers had also already had two changes of address — from Stroud Green to Weybridge, then to Hampton Court — and there would be another move, to Kennington, before the make finally expired in 1949.

'The favourite Zenith is undoubtedly the 680cc twin,' remarked *The Motor Cycle*, in describing the 1928 range, and certainly it was a size of engine that was long associated with the make, in both side-valve and overhead-valve forms. This one is the side-valve, designed as a luxury solo tourer, and for the 1928 season the luxury had been increased by the provision of a larger spring-top saddle than before (Leckie or Lycett, to choice), and by adopting the latest Druid ES-type girder front fork with enclosed centre spring. Another improvement was the mounting of the Sturmey-Archer hand gear-change lever on a bracket attached to the frame lower top rail, instead of to the actual tank.

Heavier wheels and tyres were to be standard, the latter being 3.25 × 19 in wired-edge, and the front mudguard was both wider and more deeply valanced, so enhancing the appearance and keeping road filth from the rider's legs. Though it is usual nowadays (where drum brakes are still fitted) to have a larger-diameter front brake than on the rear, on the Zenith it was the other way about, with a 6 in diameter front drum and 7 in diameter rear.

Altogether, Zenith offered nine models for 1928, ranging from a 172 cc Villiers-powered utility model, up to a choice of three 680 cc twins, the top model being the 'Super-Eight' Sports. On the track, Zenith-mounted Brooklands men were winning regularly, and Joe Wright and Oliver Baldwin, on identical 998 cc Zenith-JAP twins, were joint holders of the Brooklands track record at 113.45 until Wright finally pushed it up to 118.86 mph. With the coming of speedway, Zenith produced a JAP-engined model for the cinders, but behind the scenes things were far from well, and in 1930 the factory closed down temporarily.

The name was bought by one of Zenith's main dealers, Writers of Kennington, and production was restarted — initially at the old Hampton Court premises, but with a gradual move to Kennington. The outbreak of war again halted production, but fortunately Writers had managed to store a small supply of 750 cc vee-twin JAP engines and when peace returned the Zenith came back to the market. The last few of the batch even boasted Dowty air-sprung telescopic front forks. Sadly, JAP did not resume manufacture of vee-twin engines, once the last of Zenith's pre-war supply had been used. One prototype was built using the vertical-twin side-valve 500 cc JAP, but again JAP failed to deliver in quantity, and with no alternative four-stroke proprietary engine available, Zenith closed down permanently.

Specification

Make Zenith. **Model** 'Six-Eighty'. **Engine** JAP 680 cc (70 × 88 mm bore and stroke) 50° side-valve vee-twin. **Tyres** 3.25 × 19 in front and rear, wired edge. **Frame** Brazed-lug tubular diamond, unsprung at rear. **Front forks** Druid enclosed spring girders. **Brakes** Drums, 7 in diameter front, 8 in diameter rear. **Weight** 294 lb. **Wheelbase** 57 in. **Manufacturer** Zenith Motors Ltd, Station Road, Hampton Court, Surrey.

Above Zenith machines were always a firm favourite of the sporty crowd, and the 680 model was one of the most coveted.
Right Zeniths of the 1920s and early '30s were built at East Molesey, and the works were powered by a water turbine which drew its supplies from the River Mole.
Far right Yes — again the vee-twin JAP, and none the worse for that.
Below Surprisingly, the vee-twin Zenith survived the war, but production ceased when JAP did not go back into manufacture of big four-strokes. Purple and black was the traditional Zenith finish.

The National Motorcycle Museum

The world's only purpose-built museum complex expressly devoted to the history of the British-built motorcycle, the National Motorcycle Museum at Bickenhill — directly opposite the main entrance to the National Exhibition Centre, and right on the junction of the M42 Motorway and A45 Birmingham-Coventry trunk road — is a dream come to reality. The dreamer was Birmingham businessman Roy Richards (now the Museum's Founding Trustee), a motorcycle enthusiast who was disappointed that existing museums, with their handlebar-to-handlebar dusty and soulless line-ups, were no way to show the coming generation the kind of machines which thronged the roads in Dad's (or maybe Granddad's) day.

No, there should be a bright and airy building in which each machine would be shown to best advantage; and the machines themselves should be in sparkling, showroom condition, restored to virtually brand-new order by the best workmen available — if possible, by former employees of the factories which built the models in the first place.

Sadly, between the time that Roy Richards started his campaign to collect and restore the several hundreds of motorcycles necessary, and the eventual opening of the Museum premises, the once-dominant British two-wheel industry had shrunk to a mere shadow of its former self. But he pressed on undaunted, by now heading a charitable trust set up to administer the Museum's affairs. Fund-raising was hard work — indeed it still is, for the intention is to expand both the premises and the collection as circumstances allow — but the outcome is, as Roy had dreamed so many years ago, a true Mecca for enthusiasts, the world's finest exhibition of the British motorcycle in all its many forms.

NATIONAL MOTORCYCLE MUSEUM